Revise

Pearson Edexcel GCSE
French
Revision Workbook

Series Consultant: Harry Smith
Author: Stuart Glover

Audio for Speaking and Listening at your fingertips

Scan the green audio QR codes to immediately launch high-quality recordings of native speakers. These are exam-style tracks for realistic assessment practice and can particularly help you with:

- **Listening: Dictation task practice**
  Listen three times for exam-style practice.

- **Speaking: Read aloud practice**
  Targeted pronunciation practice of sounds helps build your confidence.

- **Speaking: Role play practice**
  Hear the teacher part and speak your answers in the pauses.

Transcripts for all audio files can be accessed here.

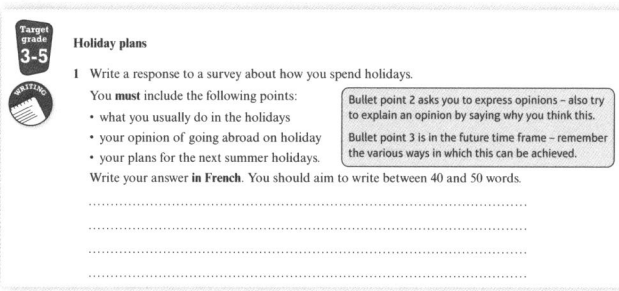

Support for longer writing tasks

Space is provided in this Workbook but sometimes you'll need to use your own paper too. Full sample student responses are given in the answer section so that you can self-assess. Remember that there is more than one correct answer for this type of question.

Practice papers

Help to check that you are exam-ready with a full set of practice papers containing exam-style questions for Speaking, Listening, Reading and Writing, for both Foundation and Higher tier.

Higher and Foundation tiers

Questions which only apply to Higher Tier are marked with an

Difficulty scale

The icon next to each exam-style question tells you how difficult it is.

Some questions cover a range of difficulties.

Target grade 4

Target grade 7-8

Also available:

The Revision Guide helps you revise vocabulary and grammar with a manageable topic-by-topic approach. Worked example questions and pages on each exam paper will build your skills ready for assessment, and digital resources such as quick quizzes, vocab checks, videos and flashcards are all included!

Pearson Edexcel publishes the only official Sample Assessment Material on its website. The questions in this Workbook have been designed to familiarise you with the type of tasks you may meet in the exam, and are tailored to help you to practise specific skills. Remember that the actual assessments may not look like this.

Contents

My people
1 Physical descriptions
2 Character descriptions
3 Friends
4 Family
5 Relationships
6 Helping friends with problems
7 When I was younger
8 Identity
9 Everyday life
10 Meals at home
11 Celebrations

Health
12 Food and drink
13 Healthy diets
14 Sport and exercise
15 Physical wellbeing
16 Mental wellbeing
17 Feeling unwell
18 Equality and sporting role models
19 Sporting events

Technology
20 Me and my mobile
21 Social media
22 The internet
23 Computer games
24 Pros and cons of technology

Free time
25 Hobbies
26 Music and dance
27 Arranging to go out
28 Reading
29 Television
30 Going to the cinema
31 Celebrity culture
32 Role models

Local environment and transport
33 Places in town
34 Things to do
35 Shopping
36 Transport
37 Travel and buying tickets
38 My region – good and bad
39 My area in the past

Tourism
40 Town or country
41 During the holidays
42 Abroad
43 Types of holiday
44 Where to stay
45 Booking accommodation
46 Holiday activities
47 Trips and excursions
48 Asking for help or directions
49 Shopping for gifts
50 Tourist information
51 Tourist attractions
52 Holiday problems
53 Accommodation problems
54 Eating out
55 Opinions about food
56 The weather
57 Customs and festivals
58 Visiting a city

My school
59 School subjects
60 School likes, dislikes and reasons
61 Timetable and school day
62 Equipment and facilities in school
63 School uniform
64 Class activities
65 School rules
66 Opinions about school
67 Clubs and activities
68 Success at school
69 Options at 16
70 Schools – France and the UK

My future
71 Future study plans
72 Future plans
73 Part-time jobs and money
74 Opinions about jobs
75 Job adverts and skills needed
76 Applying for jobs
77 Volunteering
78 Equality and helping others

Environment
79 The natural world
80 Spending time in the countryside
81 The environment and me
82 Local environmental issues
83 Global environmental issues
84 Caring for the planet
85 A greener future

About the exams
86 Practice for Paper 1: Speaking
87 Practice for Paper 1: Speaking
88 Practice for Paper 2: Listening
89 Practice for Paper 2: Listening
90 Practice for Paper 3: Reading
91 Practice for Paper 3: Reading
92 Practice for Paper 4: Writing
93 Practice for Paper 4: Writing

Grammar
94 Articles 1
95 Articles 2
96 Adjectives
97 Possessives
98 Comparisons
99 Other adjectives and pronouns
100 Adverbs
101 Object pronouns
102 More pronouns: *y* and *en*
103 Other pronouns
104 Present tense: -*er* verbs
105 Present tense: -*ir* and -*re* verbs
106 *Avoir* and *être*
107 Reflexive verbs
108 Other important verbs
109 The perfect tense 1
110 The perfect tense 2
111 The imperfect tense
112 The future tense
113 The conditional tense
114 Negatives
115 The perfect infinitive and the present participle
116 The passive
117 Questions

Practice papers
118 Speaking (Foundation)
119 Listening (Foundation)
122 Reading (Foundation)
127 Writing (Foundation)
129 Speaking (Higher)
131 Listening (Higher)
134 Reading (Higher)
139 Writing (Higher)

141 Answers

A small bit of small print
Pearson Edexcel publishes Sample Assessment Material and the Specification on its website. This is the official content and this book should be used in conjunction with it. The questions in this Workbook have been written to help you practise every topic in the book. Remember: the real exam questions may not look like this.

Had a go ☐ Nearly there ☐ Nailed it! ☐   **My people**

Physical descriptions

Descriptions

1 Read these comments from a school forum.

> **Ana:** J'ai les yeux bleus et on dit que je suis trop grande. Je n'aime pas ça. Ma meilleure amie est plus petite que moi et elle a les cheveux longs et blonds.
>
> **Lucas:** J'ai les yeux marron et les cheveux courts et noirs. Ma meilleure amie porte des lunettes et elle est plus jeune que moi.
>
> **Camille:** Je suis assez grande. J'ai les yeux verts et les cheveux roux. Ma meilleure amie est très belle. Elle a de grands yeux bleus.

Who says what? Choose the correct answers.

Put a cross [×] in the column for each correct answer.

	Who …	Ana	Lucas	Camille
(a)	… has ginger hair?			
(b)	… has a friend with blue eyes?			
(c)	… is quite tall?			
(d)	… has a friend who wears glasses?			
(e)	… has a shorter friend?			
(f)	… is very tall?			

(6 marks)

> Don't get confused between the young people and their friends. Look carefully at the subject of the sentence. Is it *je* or *mon / ma meilleur(e) ami(e)*?

> Remember *trop grand(e)* means 'too tall'.

Dictation

2 You are going to hear someone talking about themselves.

Sentences 1–3: write down the missing words in the gaps provided.
In each gap, you will write one word **in French**.

1 J'ai ………………………… yeux ………………………… .

2 Mon amie a les ………………………… noirs et ………………………… .

3 Elle ……………….. très ……………….. et ……………….. .

> In the exam you will hear each sentence three times. Here you will need to play the audio recording three times.

Sentences 4–6: write down the full sentences that you hear in the spaces provided, **in French**.

4 …………………………………………………………………………………… .

5 …………………………………………………………………………………… .

6 …………………………………………………………………………………… .

> Read the sentences first and think which type of words might work in the gaps.

(10 marks)

Listen to the recording

> Some words you will hear are not on the vocabulary list, so may be unfamiliar. Don't worry! Think of your knowledge of French sounds and how the word might be written. Even if you get it slightly wrong, as long as the French is still recognisable, a mark can still be awarded.

My people

Had a go ☐ Nearly there ☐ Nailed it! ☐

Character descriptions

General questions

1 Answer these questions about you and your friends.

> Remember to add detail: use adjectives, intensifiers like *assez* or *très* and adverbs to do this. However, don't try to use anything you don't know! Remember also to make your adjectives agree.

- Décris ton meilleur ami / ta meilleure amie.
- Tu étais comment quand tu étais plus jeune?
- Tu te fais du souci pour qui? Pourquoi?
- Qu'est-ce qui t'intéresse? Pourquoi?

> You can sometimes use material from the question itself. For example, in question 2, you might reuse *quand*, but remember to change *tu* to *je*!

Me and my friends

2 Enzo and Myriam are talking about themselves and their friends.

What do they say?

Listen to the recording and complete the sentences by putting a cross [×] in the correct box for each question.

(a) Enzo says that his friend is …

☐	**A** never funny.
☐	**B** always well-behaved.
☐	**C** very loyal.

(b) Myriam is …

☐	**A** not very sporty.
☐	**B** more hard-working than her friends.
☐	**C** never serious.

(c) People say that Enzo is …

☐	**A** funny.
☐	**B** serious.
☐	**C** not nice.

(3 marks)

> Make sure that you listen carefully, especially when people are talking about more than one person. Remember also to listen out for negatives as they can give the exact opposite meaning to something.

Had a go ☐ Nearly there ☐ Nailed it! ☐   **My people**

Friends

Read aloud

1 Your friend Sarah has sent you some information about herself.

Read out the text below.

> Always try to work out the meaning of what you are reading as this will help you.

> Remember that *j* in French is softer than English j – like the s sound in the English word 'lei**s**ure'.

> The c sound in *c'est* and *cinq* is soft, like an English s.

> *dit* and *suis* both have a silent final consonant. You pronounce them like 'dee' and 'swee'.

> *J'ai* seize ans.
> Mon anniversaire, *c'est* le cinq mai.
> Ma copine *dit* que je *suis* vraiment sympa.
> Ton frère a beaucoup de *bons* amis.
> Mes parents vont souvent *au* cinéma avec leurs voisins car ils aiment les comédies.

> *bons* would normally have a silent s at the end. However, because it is followed by a vowel in *amis*, you pronounce the s like a z – 'bonz amee'.

> Pronounce the *au* as we would in the English exclamation 'Oh!'.

> When you have finished, check your pronunciation against the sample recording in the answers section.

(8 marks)

New friends

2 Read Fathia's email to her friend, Dorian. Answer the questions **in English**. You do not need to write in full sentences.

> ✉
>
> Salut!
> Je t'écris pour te parler d'une nouvelle amie qui s'appelle Fatima. Je l'ai rencontrée à une fête il y a deux semaines. Elle me raconte des histoires amusantes et elle me fait rire. La semaine dernière, nous sommes allées en ville où nous avons fait des achats.
> J'espère que notre amitié va durer longtemps car on a les mêmes goûts.

(a) Where and when did Fathia meet Fatima? ....

.... **(2 marks)**

(b) How would you describe Fatima based on what you have read? ....

.... **(1 mark)**

(c) What did the friends do in town? .... **(1 mark)**

(d) What does Fathia hope for and why? ....

.... **(2 marks)**

> In question 2b, no adjective is used to describe Fatima, so you need to work it out from what Fathia says.

My people Had a go ☐ Nearly there ☐ Nailed it! ☐

Family

Family

1. Clara is talking about her family. What does she say?

   Listen to the recording and complete the sentences by putting a cross [×] in the correct box for each question.

   (a) Clara gets on well with …

☐	A	her father.
☐	B	her little sister.
☐	C	her mother.

   (b) Her brother is …

☐	A	hard-working.
☐	B	easy to get on with.
☐	C	difficult.

   (c) Her grandparents are …

☐	A	nice.
☐	B	strict.
☐	C	old.

   (d) They often go to the …

☐	A	cinema.
☐	B	theatre.
☐	C	beach.

   (4 marks)

Translation

2. Translate the following five sentences **into French**.

   (a) I love my family.

   ....

   (b) My father is very patient.

   ....

   (c) My mother listens to me a lot.

   ....

   (d) I am on holiday with my aunt.

   ....

   (e) Yesterday I went to the beach with my brothers.

   .... **(10 marks)**

   > Remember that the word for 'my' depends on the word it describes.
   >
   > Where will the word for 'me' come in sentence c?

Had a go ☐ Nearly there ☐ Nailed it! ☐   **My people**

Relationships

Relationships

1 Read the email that Hugo wrote to his friend.

> ✉
> Salut!
> Mon amie Ana, qui habite au Canada, m'a dit qu'elle est stressée car il y a trop de pression dans son école. Je la connais depuis douze ans et je suis vraiment triste car elle était très sympa et ouverte, mais elle ne sourit jamais, maintenant. Je lui enverrai un e-mail pour améliorer la situation.

Put a cross [×] in each one of the **three** correct boxes.

☐	A	There is too much pressure in Ana's school.
☐	B	Ana used to live in Canada.
☐	C	Hugo has known Ana for ten years.
☐	D	Ana used to be kind.
☐	E	Ana is always smiling now.
☐	F	Hugo hopes to improve the situation.

(3 marks)

> Be careful with verb tenses. There are imperfect (past), present and future tenses here to consider.

A photo of your friends

See this photo in colour

2 Describe the picture.
   Your description must cover:
   - people
   - location
   - activity.

> Make sure that you develop your answer to describe all three bullet points in relation to the picture. You should be as accurate as you can and should try to vary your vocabulary and grammar, e.g. linking your sentences and giving opinions. There is no need to use different tenses unless you want to.

(8 marks)

You must then answer two questions on the same theme.
   (a) Qu'est-ce que tu aimes faire avec tes amis?
   (b) Tu as un ou une meilleur(e) ami(e)?

(4 marks)

My people

Had a go ☐ Nearly there ☐ Nailed it! ☐

Helping friends with problems

Helping friends

1 Someone is talking about helping a friend. What do they mention?

Listen to the recording and put a cross [×] in each one of the **three** correct boxes.

☐	A	diet
☐	B	sleep
☐	C	getting up
☐	D	fitness
☐	E	homework
☐	F	medicine

(3 marks)

> When you prepare for a listening activity, try to note down the French words for the English ones so that you can listen out for them.

Dictation

2 You are going to hear someone talking about helping friends with problems.

Sentences 1–3: write down the missing words in the gaps provided. In each gap you will write one word **in French**.

1 J'aide .... mon ....

2 Mon ami ne .... pas ....

3 Maintenant il .... en ....

Sentences 4–6: write down the full sentences that you hear in the spaces provided, **in French**.

4 ....

5 ....

6 .... (10 marks)

> Make sure that you know where one word ends and the next one starts. For example, *il y a*.

> Try to translate the sentences into English, as knowing what you are writing will help.

Had a go ☐ Nearly there ☐ Nailed it! ☐   **My people**

When I was younger

Activities in the past

1 Lucas, Manon and Rachid are talking about when they were younger.

   What do they say?

   Listen to the recording and complete the following tables **in English**.

   You do not need to write in full sentences.

   (a) Lucas

Sporting activity he used to do	

   (b) Manon

Where she used to live	

   (c) Rachid

Free-time activity when younger	

   (3 marks)

   (Pay special attention to the past here, not the present.)

Conversation

2 Answer these questions about what you did when you were younger.

   > As part of a conversation, you might be asked what you were like, what you used to do and what life was like when you were younger. Remember to use the imperfect tense when you are talking about what you used to do. You can then use another tense, for example if you compare what you used to do to what you do now.

   (a) Où allais-tu en vacances quand tu étais plus jeune?
   (b) Que faisais-tu quand tu étais libre dans le passé?

My people

Had a go ☐   Nearly there ☐   Nailed it! ☐

Identity

About me

1 Write to your friend about yourself.

You **must** include the following points:
- your character and interests
- what other people think of you and why
- what you did recently with friends
- your personal future plans.

Write your answer **in French**. You should aim to write between 80 and 90 words.

....
....
....
....
....
....
....
.... **(18 marks)**

> Remember to cover all four bullet points and try to develop your sentences by linking your ideas, as this makes your sentences more complex which could earn higher marks.

Picture task: follow-up questions

2 Answer these picture task follow-up questions.

(a) Tu es quel type de personne?

(b) Quelle est ton ambition? **(4 marks)**

> You only need to communicate one sentence. In the sample answers below, there are additional, more complex sentences to give you ideas for similar questions in the conversation section (where you need to develop your answer to gain higher marks).

Had a go ☐   Nearly there ☐   Nailed it! ☐   **My people**

Everyday life

Daily routine

1 Write to your friend about your everyday life.

You **must** include the following points:
- your daily routine
- your opinion of your area with reasons
- what you did last Saturday
- where you would like to live in the future.

Write your answer **in French**. You should aim to write between 80 and 90 words.

....
....
....
....
....
....
....
....
....

(18 marks)

> Remember to cover all four bullet points and try to develop your sentences by linking your ideas, as this makes your sentences more complex and could possibly get you more marks.

Translation

2 Translate the following passage **into English**.

> Ma vie est assez simple. Après avoir passé une journée fatigante au collège, je rentre, vraiment fatigué. Auparavant je faisais mes devoirs immédiatement, mais maintenant je préfère sortir avec quelques amis. Ma ville n'est pas intéressante, alors je rêve de vivre ailleurs. Je crois que je chercherai un emploi car j'ai besoin de plus d'argent.

....
....
....
....
....
....

(10 marks)

My people — Had a go ☐ Nearly there ☐ Nailed it! ☐

Meals at home

Meals in my home

1 Write to your friend about meals at home.

You **must** include the following points:
- what you eat and drink at home
- your opinion of the food at home
- what you ate yesterday
- where you will eat or drink tomorrow.

Write your answer **in French**. You should aim to write between 80 and 90 words.

....
....
....
....
....
....
....
....
....
....
....
.... **(18 marks)**

> Remember to cover all four bullet points and try to develop your sentences by linking your ideas, as this makes your sentences more complex which should improve your marks.

> Try to stick quite closely to the suggested word count as the more you write, the more errors you might make!

Eating at home

2 Clara is talking about food at home.

What does she say?

Listen to the recording and complete the sentences by putting a cross [×] in the correct box for each question.

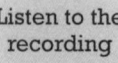

Listen to the recording

(a) Clara's family ...

☐	A always eat together.
☐	B eat when they are hungry.
☐	C always eat the same food.

(b) Yesterday Clara's sister ...

☐	A ate fish and rice.
☐	B ate at 4.45 pm.
☐	C ate earlier than Clara did.

(c) Yesterday Clara ...

☐	A did her homework as soon as she got home.
☐	B ate bread and ham.
☐	C ate at school.

(d) Clara's mother ...

☐	A made Clara some pasta.
☐	B had a glass of water.
☐	C never does the cooking.

(4 marks)

Had a go ☐   Nearly there ☐   Nailed it! ☐   **My people**

Celebrations

Picture-based task: Celebrating birthdays

See this photo in colour

1 Describe the picture. Write four short sentences **in French**.

....
....
....
.... **(8 marks)**

> When describing a photo in the Writing exam, you do not need to give complex sentences. Remember to keep it simple and only use the words you know.

A celebration

2 Toni is writing about a celebration.

> Vendredi prochain, je ferai les magasins avec mon frère au centre commercial. Je veux chercher un cadeau d'anniversaire pour ma sœur aînée qui aura bientôt dix-huit ans. Mes parents ont déjà organisé une grande fête chez nous et ils lui ont acheté une robe de marque. Je sais qu'elle voudrait bien avoir un chapeau car elle a été invitée au mariage de sa meilleure amie l'année prochaine, alors je voudrais en acheter un pour elle.

Answer the following questions **in English**. You do not need to write in full sentences.

(a) Who is going to be having a birthday soon?... **(1 mark)**

(b) What present has already been bought?... **(2 marks)**

(c) What present is Toni looking to buy?... **(1 mark)**

(d) Why?... **(1 mark)**

> When there are 2 marks available, there will be more than one element to the answer, as in question 2 here.

Health — Had a go ☐ Nearly there ☐ Nailed it! ☐

Food and drink

The food I eat

1 Write to your friend about food and drink.

You **must** include the following points:
- what you normally eat for breakfast
- your favourite food and why you like it
- a meal you ate whilst on holiday in the past
- a dish you'd like to try in the future.

Write your answer **in French**. You should aim to write between 80 and 90 words.

....
....
....
....
....
....
....
....
....
....
....
....
....
....
.... **(18 marks)**

> Checklist: Use three time frames, give opinions and reasons, and use longer sentences!

Conversation

2 Answer the following question **in French**.

(a) Qu'est-ce que tu aimes boire? Pourquoi?

> This question could form part of the conversation in the Speaking exam.

> Check your response to this question against those given in the Answer section. Two sample answers are given: a simple answer and an improved one which would help you gain a higher grade.

12

Had a go ☐ Nearly there ☐ Nailed it! ☐

Health

Healthy diets

Dictation

1 You are going to hear someone talking about food.

   Sentences 1–2: write down the missing words in the gaps provided. In each gap you will write one word **in French**.

   1 J'aime les ...., les .... et les ....

   2 Mes .... préférés sont les .... et les ....

   Sentences 3 to 6: write down the full sentences that you hear in the spaces provided, **in French**.

   3 ....
   4 ....
   5 ....
   6 ....   **(10 marks)**

> Remember that some words sound the same in both singular and plural but have different spellings at the end. Pay close attention to which you need.

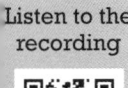

My diet

2 Théo has written an entry in his diary about healthy diets.

   Put a cross [×] next to each one of the **three** correct statements.

> Je sais que si on ne mange pas bien, on aura des problèmes de santé graves et inquiétants plus tard.
>
> Malgré ça, hier soir, j'ai commandé un repas malsain au restaurant. Mes copains m'ont dit de limiter ma consommation de frites, mais c'est vraiment difficile car je les trouve vraiment savoureuses.
>
> À l'avenir, je vais essayer de suivre un régime plus sain.

☐	A	Théo knows that eating unhealthy food will cause serious problems.
☐	B	Théo ordered a healthy meal yesterday.
☐	C	Théo's friends have warned him to eat fewer chips.
☐	D	Théo doesn't like the taste of chips.
☐	E	Théo is going to try to eat more healthy food in the future.
☐	F	Théo has begun to eat more healthily.

(3 marks)

> Make sure you put a cross against the required number of answers for a question. In this case, you need three.

Health

Had a go ☐ Nearly there ☐ Nailed it! ☐

Sport and exercise

Role play

1 **Setting: Leisure centre**

Scenario:
- You are at a leisure centre in France.
- Listen to the recording of the teacher's part.
- Your teacher will play the part of an employee at the leisure centre and will speak first.
- Your teacher will ask questions **in French** and you must answer **in French**.
- You are expected to say a few words or a short phrase / sentence in response to each prompt. One-word answers will not be sufficient to gain full marks.

Task:
1 Say what activity you want to do at the leisure centre.
2 Say how many people it's for.
3 Tell the employee what your plans are for this evening.
4 Ask a question about closing times.
5 Ask a question about cost.

(10 marks)

The teacher will use the formal register (*vous*) in the speaking role play, but you can reply in the informal register (*tu*) and this is still acceptable.

A gym review

2 Write a review of a gym for a website.

You **must** include the following points:
- where the gym is
- your opinion of the gym
- when you will next visit the gym.

Write your answer **in French**. You should aim to write between 40 and 50 words.

....
....
....
....
....
....
....
....

(14 marks)

Make sure that you cover all three bullet points and develop some of your ideas to get higher marks, for example by justifying your response or giving an opinion. Try to use a bit of variety in your vocabulary and phrases, for example by linking your ideas.

Had a go ☐ Nearly there ☐ Nailed it! ☐   **Health**

Physical wellbeing

Read aloud

1 Your friend Dorian has sent you some information about himself.

Read out the text below.

> Je suis actif.
> Je fais du vélo le week-end.
> Je joue au tennis avec mes amis chaque vendredi soir.
> Je ne suis pas souvent malade.
> Il est important de bien manger et de boire de l'eau.

> When you have finished, check your pronunciation against the sample recording in the Answers section.

Follow-on questions

Once you have read the text aloud, answer these two questions related to what you have read.

You are expected to say a few words or a short phrase / sentence in response to each question.

One-word answers will not be sufficient to gain full marks.

(a) Qu'est-ce que tu aimes boire?

(b) Que penses-tu du sport? **(Total 12 marks)**

> Listen to the recording to help you understand how to say some of these French sounds.
> - *suis* normally has a silent final consonant. However, here it is followed by a vowel in *actif*, so you pronounce the s to make it easier to say. This is the same for *mes amis* – you pronounce the s of *mes*.
> - The a sounds in *malade* are short, like in the English 'address'.
> - i in *il* is long, like ee.
> - The an in *important* is a bit like the o in the English 'orange'.

Track 10

Physical fitness

2 Ahmed has sent an email to his friend about physical fitness.

> ✉
> J'ai l'intention d'améliorer ma forme car je voudrais avoir du succès sportif. J'ai essayé plusieurs sports d'équipe, mais ils ne m'intéressent pas car je les trouve difficiles et un peu **barbants**. Alors, je préfère pratiquer un sport où on peut réussir seul comme le tennis ou l'athlétisme.
> La semaine prochaine, je vais commencer à m'entraîner dans un club sportif en ville. Je rêve de devenir plus sain.

Answer the following questions **in English**.

(a) What does Ahmed intend to do and why? .... **(2 marks)**

(b) What kind of sport does he prefer? .... **(1 mark)**

(c) What will he do next week? .... **(1 mark)**

(d) Which of these is the best translation of *barbants*? **(1 mark)**

☐ **A** lonely   ☐ **B** boring   ☐ **C** interesting

> When you have to work out the meaning of a word which is not in the vocabulary list for the examination, look carefully at the sentence in which the word is found. Try to translate the words around it to have a reasoned guess at the meaning if you don't know.

| Health | Had a go ☐ Nearly there ☐ Nailed it! ☐ |

Mental wellbeing

Conversation

1. Answer the following questions **in French**.

   (a) Que penses-tu de la santé mentale?

   (b) Quels sont les dangers pour les jeunes?

   > You might be asked questions like these in the conversation task.

Translation

2. Translate the following five sentences **into French**.

   (a) I am sad.

   ....

   (b) My friend cannot sleep.

   > In sentence (b), remember where to put *ne ... pas*.

   ....

   (c) Mental health is important.

   > You need to use *La* to start sentence (c).

   ....

   (d) I think that I have too many exams and I am stressed.

   ....

   (e) Last week I started to do more sport to help my mental health.

   .... **(10 marks)**

   > Use *trop de* in sentence (d) and *plus de* in sentence (e).

Had a go ☐ Nearly there ☐ Nailed it! ☐   **Health**

Feeling unwell

Picture-based task: Feeling unwell

See this photo in colour

1 Describe the picture. Write four short sentences **in French**.

....

....

....

.... **(8 marks)**

> For the picture task, be sure to keep your answers very clear and simple. There is no need to write complex sentences, but make sure you include a verb in each one.

Illness and injury

2 Morgane has sent an email to her friend about illness and injury.

> ✉
>
> Il y a beaucoup de problèmes chez nous. Hier, ma grande sœur s'est coupé le doigt en préparant le repas du soir, et elle a dû aller à l'hôpital. Cependant, ce n'était pas trop grave.
>
> Ce matin, après m'être levée, j'avais mal à la tête et ma mère m'a dit que j'avais aussi de la fièvre. Je ne suis pas allée au lycée et j'ai passé la journée au lit.

Put a cross [×] next to each one of the **three** correct statements.

☐	A	Morgane's sister cut her finger last week.
☐	B	Morgane had to go to hospital.
☐	C	Morgane's sister's injury was not too serious.
☐	D	Morgane had a headache this morning.
☐	E	Morgane's mother had a fever.
☐	F	Morgane spent a day in bed.

(3 marks)

> Pay special attention to the people involved and the times mentioned.

Health

Had a go ☐ Nearly there ☐ Nailed it! ☐

Equality and sporting role models

Target grade 1-5

Translation

1 Translate the following five sentences **into French**.

(a) Equality is very important.

....

(b) I respect a lot of sporting celebrities.

....

(c) I think that I can help people.

....

(d) I don't want to be rich or famous.

....

(e) Last week I watched my role model on television.

.... **(10 marks)**

> Make sure that adjectives like *important* and *sportif* agree in sentences (a) and (b).

> Don't forget the definite article 'the', which is needed in French with words like 'equality' and 'television'.

Target grade 6-8

Equality in sport

2 Alessandro is talking about equality and sport.

What does he say?

Listen to the podcast and put a cross [×] in each one of the **three** correct boxes.

☐	A	A group is going to be organised at school against discrimination.
☐	B	In the past, girls couldn't play in football matches.
☐	C	The group is concerned only with sport.
☐	D	The group is concerned about bullying.
☐	E	There is going to be a worldwide event.
☐	F	Alessandro hopes that everyone will have fun in the future.

(3 marks)

> Make sure you put a cross against the required number of answers for a question. In this case, you need three.

Had a go ☐   **Nearly there** ☐   **Nailed it!** ☐   **Health**

Sporting events

Picture-based task: Watching a sporting event

1 Describe the picture. Write four short sentences **in French**.

....

....

....

.... **(8 marks)**

> Remember, you don't need to add lots of detail in complex sentences for this particular task.

Translation

2 Translate the following paragraph **into English**.

> J'adore regarder le sport à la télé et je vais souvent à des événements sportifs. Récemment, ma copine m'a invité à regarder le Tour de France puisqu'elle savait qu'on s'amuserait bien. J'ai trouvé le concours intéressant, mais il a plu toute la journée. L'année prochaine, j'irai regarder un match de football professionnel. Après le mauvais temps qu'on a eu pour le vélo, j'espère qu'il fera plus beau pour le football !

....

....

....

.... **(10 marks)**

> Make sure that you translate using correct tenses. Make a list of the verbs using these headings.
>
> There are some examples already filled in.
>
> | Present | Perfect | Imperfect | Future | Conditional |
> |---------|---------|-----------|--------|-------------|
> | J'adore | J'ai trouvé | Elle savait | J'irai | On s'amuserait |
>
> Remember that the French often use *on* when the English would use 'we'.

Technology

Had a go ☐ Nearly there ☐ Nailed it! ☐

Me and my mobile

Picture-based task: Mobile phones

1 Describe the picture.

Your description **must** cover:
- people
- location
- activity.

(8 marks)

Follow-on questions

When you have finished your description, listen to the recording of two questions relating to the picture. You are expected to say a few words or a short phrase / sentence in response to each question. One-word answers will not be sufficient to gain full marks.

(4 marks)

> Even at Higher tier, in the picture task you just have to talk about people, location and activity clearly. Keep your answers to the two follow-on questions simple too; there are only two marks available per question.

My mobile phone

2 Read these comments from an internet forum.

> **Alex:** Je parle avec mes amis sur mon portable et on discute de musique.
>
> **Toni:** Je n'aime pas envoyer des messages et des e-mails, mais de temps en temps je partage des photos et je télécharge de la musique.
>
> **Jade:** Mon frère m'envoie souvent des e-mails sur mon portable. J'aime vraiment regarder des vidéos amusantes.

Who says what? Choose the correct answers.

Put a cross [×] in the correct column for each question.

	Who …	Alex	Toni	Jade
(a)	… likes watching funny things?			
(b)	… talks about music?			
(c)	… receives emails often?			
(d)	… does not like sending emails?			
(e)	… talks to friends on a mobile?			
(f)	… shares photos?			

(6 marks)

> Be careful as *musique* and *e-mails* appear in the comments of two different people.

Had a go ☐   Nearly there ☐   Nailed it! ☐   **Technology**

Social media

Conversation

1 Answer these questions about your attitude to social media.

(a) Que penses-tu des réseaux sociaux?

(b) Tu passes beaucoup de temps en ligne chaque jour? Pourquoi?

> These questions could be part of a general conversation topic.

> To get higher marks, try to include some constructions which require the use of the infinitive like *on peut* … ('you can …').

Social media

2 Read Charlie's email to Manon.

> ✉
>
> Je passe beaucoup de temps sur les réseaux sociaux et je pense que ma tablette et mon portable sont essentiels dans ma vie quotidienne. Cependant, je sais qu'il y a des dangers comme le harcèlement et la cybercriminalité. Pourtant, je trouve que c'est un moyen efficace de suivre les événements mondiaux. Par exemple, hier, j'ai regardé une vidéo intéressante sur Instagram sur l'aide pour les pauvres à Madagascar.
>
> Demain je vais partager une photo amusante de mon chien et tous mes amis vont sourire.

Answer the following questions **in English**. You do not need to write in full sentences.

(a) What does Charlie say about his tablet and his mobile?

.... **(2 marks)**

(b) What two dangers does he mention?

.... **(2 marks)**

(c) What did he watch yesterday?

.... **(2 marks)**

(d) What will his friends do tomorrow?

.... **(1 mark)**

> Read the whole passage through carefully at least once before trying to answer the questions. It will help you get a sense of the content and might help you to avoid making mistakes.

Technology — Had a go ☐ Nearly there ☐ Nailed it! ☐

The internet

Dictation

1 You are going to hear someone talking about the internet.

Sentences 1–3: write down the missing words in the gaps provided. In each gap you will write one word **in French**.

1 Mon .... déteste ....
2 En ligne j'......................... de la musique ....
3 J'aime .... des .... chères.

Sentences 4–6: write down the full sentences that you hear in the spaces provided, **in French**.

4 ....
5 ....
6 ....

> Listen carefully to whether any of the missing words will need a feminine or plural ending for example.

> Try to be accurate, but you might get rewarded for a word, even if there is a slight error, so don't give up!

(10 marks)

A laptop review

2 Write a review of your laptop computer for a website.

You **must** include the following points:
- what your laptop looks like
- your opinion of your laptop
- how you will use the internet next week.

Write your answer **in French**. You should aim to write between 40 and 50 words.

> Make sure that you cover all three bullet points with some development of ideas as clearly as you can. Don't use something that you are unsure about as this might lose you marks.

....
....
....
....
....
....
....
....

(14 marks)

22

Had a go ☐ Nearly there ☐ Nailed it! ☐   **Technology**

Computer games

Picture-based task: Video games

1 Describe the picture. Your description must cover:
   - people
   - location
   - activity.

When you have finished your description, listen to the recording of two questions relating to the picture.

You are expected to say a few words or a short phrase / sentence in response to each question. One-word answers will not be sufficient to gain full marks.

> Remember to focus your picture description on the three elements given: people, location and activity. You don't need to add anything else complex.

See this photo in colour

(12 marks)

Computer games blog

2 Read Jules's blog about computer games.

> Mon loisir préféré, c'est les jeux vidéo. Hier, j'ai acheté de nouveaux écouteurs que je vais utiliser pour la première fois ce soir. Ils étaient chers! Je suis membre d'un club virtuel où on peut essayer des jeux avant de les acheter ou de les télécharger ailleurs. À mon avis, ça vaut la peine d'être membre car l'abonnement ne coûte pas beaucoup.

Complete the sentences below.

Put a cross [×] in the correct box for each question.

(a) Jules's headphones are …

☐	**A** old.
☐	**B** expensive.
☐	**C** nearly new.

(b) He has …

☐	**A** not used them yet.
☐	**B** used them once.
☐	**C** used them last night.

(c) At his virtual club you can …

☐	**A** download games.
☐	**B** try out games.
☐	**C** buy games.

(d) He thinks that the club is …

☐	**A** good value.
☐	**B** too expensive.
☐	**C** a bad idea.

(4 marks)

> If there are words or phrases that you don't know, read carefully around them as there will be clues from the words that you do know.

Technology

Had a go ☐ Nearly there ☐ Nailed it! ☐

Pros and cons of technology

Staying safe online

1. Lucas, Fathia and Inès are talking about technology.

   What do they say?

   Listen to the recording and complete the following tables **in English**.

   You do not need to write in full sentences.

   (a) Lucas

How to be safer online	

   (b) Fathia

Disadvantage of technology	

   (c) Inès

Her parents' rule	

   (3 marks)

   > Look at the English words in the table and try to think what they are in French so you can listen for some of them during the recording.

Technology blog

2. Dorian has written a blog about technology.

   > Avant, je pensais qu'il n'y avait que des avantages à la technologie. J'utilisais ma tablette sans problèmes et je jouais et discutais avec mes copains en ligne. Cependant, il y a trois jours, quelqu'un m'a envoyé des messages qui n'étaient pas agréables. J'ai parlé avec mes parents car j'étais un peu inquiet. Maintenant, je sais qu'il y a aussi des inconvénients à la technologie et je serai plus conscient de la sécurité en ligne.

   Put a cross [×] next to each one of the **three** correct statements.

☐	A	Dorian used to think that there were no disadvantages of technology.
☐	B	Dorian had lots of problems using his tablet in the past.
☐	C	Dorian received unpleasant messages three weeks ago.
☐	D	Dorian has changed his mind about technology.
☐	E	Dorian hopes to make more friends online in the future.
☐	F	Dorian is going to be more aware of online safety.

   (3 marks)

   > Always check carefully how many statements you need to choose. Here you need three.

Had a go ☐ Nearly there ☐ Nailed it! ☐   **Free time**

Hobbies

Your hobbies

1 Write to your friend about hobbies.

You **must** include the following points:
- some hobbies popular with young people
- your favourite hobby with reasons
- your activities last weekend
- what you will do next week.

Write your answer **in French**. You should aim to write between 80 and 90 words.

> Make sure that you check each bullet point to make sure that you know which time frame to use.

....
....
....
....
....
....
....

(18 marks)

My hobby

2 Marie has written this diary entry.

> J'ai un nouveau loisir que j'adore. Je suis membre d'un club dans une ville à un kilomètre de chez moi, ce qui n'est pas trop loin. Mes amis jouent de la guitare et moi, je chante. Nous avons commencé à jouer ensemble. C'était difficile au début, mais maintenant, c'est plus facile. Le mois prochain, nous allons jouer à la fête d'anniversaire de mon oncle.

Complete the sentences below.

Put a cross [×] in the correct box for each question.

(a) Marie has …

☐	A	a new hobby.
☐	B	always wanted to sing.
☐	C	started to play guitar.

(b) The club she goes to is …

☐	A	in her home town.
☐	B	quite close to where she lives.
☐	C	10 kilometres away from her home.

(c) She says that performing …

☐	A	has got easier.
☐	B	is very difficult.
☐	C	has got harder.

(d) Next month she is going to …

☐	A	have a birthday party.
☐	B	sing at a wedding.
☐	C	perform at a birthday celebration.

(4 marks)

> Read the options carefully and don't rush to assume that if a word is in the text, it is the correct answer. In part (d) here, *anniversaire* appears in the text, but 'birthday' appears in two of the options.

Free time

Had a go □ Nearly there □ Nailed it! □

Music and dance

Picture-based task: Dancing with friends

See this photo in colour

Marks are awarded for simple, clear and relevant information about what is in the picture. There are only two marks awarded for each sentence, so a short, correct phrase is all that is necessary for each.

1 Describe the picture. Write four short sentences **in French**.

....

....

....

....

(8 marks)

Role play

2 **Setting: Concert booking office**

Scenario:
- You are at a concert booking office in France with a friend.
- Listen to the recording of the teacher's part.
- The teacher will play the part of the employee and will speak first.
- The teacher will ask questions **in French** and you must answer **in French**.
- You are expected to say a few words or a short phrase / sentence in response to each prompt. One-word answers will not be sufficient to gain full marks.

Task:
1 Say what type of concert you want to watch.
2 Ask about the cost of a ticket.
3 Say that you are paying.
4 Say where you will go after the concert.
5 Ask a question about the end of the concert.

(10 marks)

The teacher will use the formal register (*vous*) in the speaking role play, but you can reply in the informal register (*tu*) and this is still acceptable.

Try to communicate as clearly as you can but remember that a short, correct sentence each time is all that is required.

Had a go ☐ Nearly there ☐ Nailed it! ☐   **Free time**

Arranging to go out

Read aloud

1 Your French penfriend, Clara, has sent you a text about going out.

Read out the text below, then listen to the recording in the Answer section to check your pronunciation.

> J'aime beaucoup sortir.
> J'ai un groupe de bons amis.
> On va souvent en ville.
> Il y a une grande piscine.
> Quand il fait beau, je vais au parc pour rencontrer mes amis et jouer au football.

(8 marks)

Track 17

Listen to the recording to help you practise some key French sounds that are useful here.
- j in *j'aime* is soft like the s sound in 'leisure'
- silent final consonants like in *beaucoup* – the p is not pronounced
- ou in *beaucoup* is like the 'oo' sound in 'shoe' (but shorter!)
- But when a silent final consonant is followed by a vowel, you pronounce it! *bons amis* (bonzami).
- The French r is soft and said at the back of the throat.

Unable to go out

2 Hugo has sent you an email.

> ✉
>
> Hier soir, mon meilleur copain, Jules, m'a invité à sortir avec lui car il y avait un festival de musique au château près de chez moi. Je voulais y aller, mais j'ai dû rester à la maison pour garder mon petit frère, alors je lui ai dit que je ne pouvais pas l'accompagner.
>
> Lui, il est allé au festival avec un groupe d'amis et ils m'ont envoyé beaucoup de photos de ce qui s'est passé là. Il y avait une foule énorme et on m'a dit que tout le monde semblait être vraiment heureux.

Complete the gap in each sentence using a word or phrase from the box below. There are more words / phrases than gaps.

> by his best friend   by his brother   by his sister
> near Hugo's house   near a castle   in a garden
> go out with his little brother   stay at home   rest
> photos   a message   a letter
> a house   a crowd   a band

(a) Hugo was invited to go out ....
(b) The festival took place ....
(c) Hugo had to ....
(d) Hugo received ....
(e) At the festival there was ....   **(5 marks)**

> Read the passage through carefully at least once to get the overall meaning before looking at the questions. It might help you to avoid making simple mistakes.

Free time — Had a go ☐ Nearly there ☐ Nailed it! ☐

Reading

Target grade 1-5

Translation

1. Translate the following five sentences **into French**.

   (a) I love reading.

   ....

   (b) My sister reads every day if she has the time.

   ....

   (c) I think that books are interesting.

   ....

   (d) Last week I bought a newspaper in town.

   ....

   (e) I want to read more often.

   .... **(10 marks)**

   > In sentence (a) you could translate this as 'to read' or 'reading'. If you choose 'reading', you will need to use *la*.
   >
   > In sentence (c), 'interesting' is an adjective which will have to change its spelling to agree with 'books'.
   >
   > In sentence (d), 'bought' will need *j'ai*.

Target grade 6-8

My recent reading

2. Luis has sent you an email about reading.

   > ✉
   >
   > Avant, je n'aimais pas lire car je pensais que ce n'était pas intéressant et je préférais mon ordinateur, mais récemment, j'ai lu un roman qui m'a vraiment touché. Le roman raconte l'histoire d'un homme qui n'avait pas d'argent et qui a essayé d'améliorer sa vie, sans succès. Après avoir lu le livre, j'ai pleuré!

   Put a cross [×] next to each one of the **three** correct statements.

☐	A	Luis has always liked reading.
☐	B	Luis used to read novels.
☐	C	He recently read a novel which had an effect on him.
☐	D	He mentions the storyline of a novel.
☐	E	Luis has tried to improve his life.
☐	F	Luis found a book he read sad.

   (3 marks)

   > You sometimes have to make a connection between words in statements and words in the passage by inference.

Had a go ☐ Nearly there ☐ Nailed it! ☐   **Free time**

Television

Watching television

1 Clara has sent you an email about television.

> ✉
>
> Je ne regarde que les émissions de science-fiction car je les trouve passionnantes. Ma meilleure copine s'intéresse aux séries et elle les regarde le lundi, le mardi et le mercredi. Elle en parle sans cesse et je trouve ça triste parce qu'elle devrait sortir plus !
>
> La semaine dernière, elle regardait sa série préférée quand j'ai changé de chaîne … Et elle n'était pas contente !
>
> J'espère qu'elle va devenir plus active à l'avenir.

Complete the sentences below.

Put a cross [×] in the correct box for each question.

(a) Clara doesn't watch …

☐ A anything but science fiction programmes.
☐ B TV.
☐ C science fiction programmes.

(b) Her friend …

☐ A watches soap operas three times a week.
☐ B loves science fiction programmes.
☐ C watches TV rarely.

(c) Clara thinks her friend …

☐ A changes channels too much.
☐ B is not happy.
☐ C should be more active.

(3 marks)

Views on television

2 Nathan is talking about television.

What does he say?

Listen to the recording and answer the following questions **in English**.

1 What did Nathan's father use to do? (Give **two** details.) ....
.... **(2 marks)**

2 What does Nathan prefer to watch on TV? .... **(1 mark)**

3 What does he not watch? .... **(1 mark)**

> When there are negatives involved, make sure you are answering the correct question.

> Make sure you listen right to the end of the recording before writing your answer.

 **Free time**

Had a go ☐   Nearly there ☐   Nailed it! ☐

Going to the cinema

Role play

1   Setting: **At the cinema**

   Scenario:
   - You are at a cinema in France.
   - Listen to the recording of the teacher's part.
   - The teacher will play the part of an employee and will speak first.
   - The teacher will ask questions **in French** and you must answer **in French**.
   - You are expected to say a few words or a short phrase / sentence in response to each prompt. One-word answers will not be sufficient to gain full marks.

   > **Task:**
   > 1 Say what type of film you want to watch.
   > 2 Ask about the price for students.
   > 3 Say why you like going to the cinema.
   > 4 Say something about a recent film you watched.
   > 5 Ask a question about food and / or drink at the cinema.

   (10 marks)

   > Remember how to ask a question. You could use *Est-ce que*, or put your voice up at the end of the sentence. You could also use a question phrase like *C'est combien … ?* or use a question word like *Où* or *Quand*.

Writing about going out

2   Write to your friend about going out.

   You **must** include the following points:
   - where you go out
   - your opinion of the local cinema with reasons
   - what you did last weekend when you went out
   - what film you would like to see in the future.

   Write your answer **in French**. You should aim to write between 80 and 90 words.

   ....

   ....

   ....

   ....

   ....

   ....

   ....

   ....

   (18 marks)

Had a go ☐ **Nearly there** ☐ **Nailed it!** ☐   Free time

Celebrity culture

Who likes celebrities?

1 Lucas is talking about celebrities.

What does he say?

Complete the gap in each sentence using a word or phrase from the box below.

There are more words / phrases than gaps.

> forget problems   read about problems   be informed
> acting   fashion   photography
> famous   rich   fashionable

(a) Lucas reads articles on celebrities to ....

(b) Fathia loves..

(c) Lucas's brother thinks celebrities don't deserve to be ....

(3 marks)

Translation

2 Translate the following sentences **into English**.

(a) J'aime regarder les célébrités à la télévision.

....

(b) Mon acteur préféré est très amusant.

....

(c) Si j'ai le temps, je lis des articles sur des chanteurs.

....

(d) La semaine dernière je suis allé à un concert.

....

(e) Mes parents ne s'intéressent jamais aux personnes célèbres.

....

(10 marks)

> In sentence (b) *préféré* is an adjective.

> In sentence (d), make sure you use the correct tense.

Free time

Had a go ☐ Nearly there ☐ Nailed it! ☐

Role models

Celebrity role models

1 Camille is talking about celebrity role models.

What does she say about her role model?

Listen to the recording and put a cross [×] in each one of the **three** correct boxes.

☐	**A**	He is rich.
☐	**B**	He likes going to the cinema.
☐	**C**	He is famous in many countries.
☐	**D**	He recently opened a cinema.
☐	**E**	He is open.
☐	**F**	He is honest.

> Vincent Cassel is a French actor.

(3 marks)

> Don't worry if there are a few words you don't recognise. Use the words around them to try to work out any meanings.

Translation

2 Translate the paragraph **into French**.

> I like singing very much. My favourite artist is famous in France and last year I went to see her in a concert. It was the best night of my life! She inspires me because she is kind and patient. I'm going to listen to her new song online next week and I hope it will be great.

> 'Singing' will be an infinitive in French.

> 'Her' and 'me' are direct object pronouns and they must come before the verb in French.

....
....
....
....
....
....
....
....
....
....

(10 marks)

Had a go ☐ Nearly there ☐ Nailed it! ☐   **Local environment and transport**

Places in town

My town

1 Chloé is talking about her town.

Answer the questions **in English**. You do not need to write in full sentences.

> Avant, ma ville était plus petite et il n'y avait ni bibliothèque ni gymnase, mais maintenant, on peut emprunter des livres et faire des activités sportives sans quitter la ville. Ma ville me plaît, surtout car on vient de faire construire une nouvelle piscine et tous mes copains y vont afin de se rencontrer et de faire de la natation.
>
> Même si j'aime bien ma région, je crois que je vais vivre ailleurs à l'avenir parce que j'ai l'intention de passer du temps à l'étranger.

(a) What did Chloé's town not use to have?

.... **(2 marks)**

(b) What particular reason does Chloé give for liking her town now?

.... **(1 mark)**

(c) Where does she intend to spend time in the future?

.... **(1 mark)**

My area

2 Write about your area for an online magazine.

You **must** include the following points:
- what makes a good town / region
- the pros and cons of where you live
- what you did in your area recently
- where you will live in the future.

> Try to include as many of the following as you can to score higher marks:
>
> Adjectives, adverbs, pronouns, different time frames, connectives and different subjects of the verb.

Write your answer **in French**. You should aim to write between 130 and 150 words.

....
....
....
....
....
....
....
....
....
....

(22 marks)

Local environment and transport

Had a go ☐   Nearly there ☐   Nailed it! ☐

Things to do

What I like to do

1 Read what Diane has written in an email to her friend.

✉
J'ai beaucoup de loisirs. J'aime bien faire du vélo à la campagne de temps en temps, mais je préfère rester en ville où on peut aller faire les magasins et il y a beaucoup de cafés et de restaurants. Hier, j'ai pris un repas excellent avec ma famille avant d'aller au cinéma. Le film qu'on a vu était triste, mais je l'ai bien aimé. Demain, je vais encore aller en ville parce que je vais rencontrer mes copains et nous allons passer du temps ensemble et parler.

(3 marks)

> For sentences which contain multiple ideas or clauses, make sure you are clear which part is relevant to the question. For example, Diane's second sentence mentions lots of things she likes doing, but only one will correctly answer question (a).

Complete the sentences below.

Put a cross [×] in the correct box for each question.

(a) Diane likes being in town because …

☐ **A** she likes going cycling.
☐ **B** you can go shopping.
☐ **C** it's relaxing.

(b) Yesterday she …

☐ **A** watched a sad film.
☐ **B** had a meal with friends.
☐ **C** didn't enjoy her trip to the cinema.

(c) Tomorrow she is going to …

☐ **A** go to the cinema.
☐ **B** talk to her friends.
☐ **C** meet her best friend.

Translation

2 Translate the following five sentences **into French**.

(a) I love sport.

....

(b) I like going shopping in town.

....

> In sentence (b) 'going' will be *faire*.

(c) In my neighbourhood you can visit the market.

....

> In sentence (c) 'visit' will be *visiter*.

(d) Yesterday I went cycling with my friends.

....

> In sentence (d) 'I went' will be *j'ai fait* not *je suis allé*.

(e) On Thursday I'm going to see a film with my sister and aunt.

....

> In sentence (e) 'I'm going' will be *je vais*.

(10 marks)

34

Had a go ☐ **Nearly there** ☐ **Nailed it!** ☐   **Local environment and transport**

Shopping

Dictation

1. You are going to hear someone talking about shopping.

   Sentences 1–3: write down the missing words in the gaps provided. In each gap, you will write one word **in French**.

   1 Ma mère .... aux ....

   2 Elle .... acheter des ....

   3 J' .... une ....

   > There will be two words (here two items of clothing) which are not in the vocabulary list. Try to work out how to spell them from what you hear.

   Sentences 4–6: write down the full sentences that you hear in the spaces provided, **in French**.

   4 ....

   5 ....

   6 ....   **(10 marks)**

Role play

2. **Setting: In a clothes shop**

   Scenario:
   - You are in a clothes shop in France with a friend.
   - Listen to the recording of the teacher's part.
   - The teacher will play the part of the employee and will speak first.
   - The teacher will ask questions **in French** and you must answer **in French**.
   - You are expected to say a few words or a short phrase / sentence in response to each prompt. One-word answers will not be sufficient to gain full marks.

   > **Task:**
   > 1 Say what item of clothing you want.
   > 2 Say what size you'd like.
   > 3 Ask how much the item costs.
   > 4 Say what you are going to buy tomorrow.
   > 5 Ask a question about closing times of the shop.

   (10 marks)

   > Remember that you can form a future time frame by using the present tense of *aller* + infinitive.

Local environment and transport

Had a go ☐   Nearly there ☐   Nailed it! ☐

Transport

Picture-based task: On a train

1 Describe the picture.

Your description **must** cover:
- people
- location
- activity. **(8 marks)**

Follow-on questions

When you have finished your description, listen to the recording of two questions relating to the picture. You are expected to say a few words or a short phrase / sentence in response to each question. One-word answers will not be sufficient to gain full marks. **(4 marks)**

Ways of travelling

2 Myriam and Théo are talking about the advantages and disadvantages of different means of transport.

What do they say?

Listen to the podcast and complete the following tables **in English**.

You do not need to write in full sentences.

(a) Myriam

Disadvantage:	
Advantage:	

(b) Théo

Advantage:	
Disadvantage:	

(4 marks)

Make sure that you don't confuse advantages and disadvantages!

Had a go ☐   Nearly there ☐   Nailed it! ☐   **Local environment and transport**

Travel and buying tickets

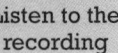

Role play

1 **Setting: At a train station**

   Scenario:
   - You are at a train station in France.
   - Listen to the recording of the teacher's part.
   - The teacher will play the part of an employee at the train station and will speak first.
   - The teacher will ask questions **in French** and you must answer **in French**.
   - You are expected to say a few words or a short phrase / sentence in response to each prompt. One-word answers will not be sufficient to gain full marks.

   Task:
   1 Say what ticket you want.
   2 Say who you are travelling with.
   3 Tell the employee your favourite means of transport.
   4 Tell the employee what you think about the café at the station.
   5 Ask a question about the time of the train.

   (10 marks)

   > Remember that to ask a question, you might need a question word or phrase. Here it's *A quelle heure … ?*

   > It's a good idea to learn some simple phrases so that you can express a quick opinion on something: *C'est génial* ('it's great'); *C'est terrible* ('it's awful'); *C'est nul(le)* ('it's rubbish'); *Ce n'est pas mal* ('it's not bad'); *C'est excellent* ('it's excellent').

Travel experiences

2 Nadia has written a blog about travel.

   > Je vais aller au Canada la semaine prochaine et je suis assez inquiète car je n'ai jamais voyagé sans ma famille et j'ai peur des avions. Je suis allée en Angleterre l'année dernière et c'était assez difficile parce qu'il y avait un retard de trois heures à l'aéroport.
   > J'espère que tout ira bien, mais maintenant je dois faire ma valise !

   What does Nadia say?

   Put a cross [×] next to each one of the **three** correct statements.

☐	A	Nadia is anxious about travelling by plane.
☐	B	Nadia often travels without her family.
☐	C	Nadia went to Canada last month.
☐	D	Nadia has had travel problems before.
☐	E	Her trip to England was not difficult.
☐	F	She is going to pack her suitcase.

   (3 marks)

   > Passages like this sometimes need you to recognise the tenses of the verbs and the time indicators.

| Local environment and transport | Had a go ☐ Nearly there ☐ Nailed it! ☐ |

My region – good and bad

Talking about my region

1 As part of a conversation topic, you might talk about your region. Speak for about 30 seconds on this question:

   (a) Quels sont les avantages et les inconvénients de ta région?

   > This is an example of a question about where you live, which you might be asked in a conversation.

   > Try to add different time frames to add complexity and variety.

A blog about my region

2 Rachid has written a blog about where he lives.

> Ma région se trouve dans le nord de la France et je la trouve vraiment géniale. Je vis dans une petite ville, mais il n'y a pas trop de circulation et les rues sont propres. On peut faire les magasins et il y a beaucoup d'activités sportives à faire aussi.
>
> Malheureusement, il y a quelquefois des festivals et il y a trop de bruit, surtout le soir. Je voudrais continuer d'habiter ici à l'avenir.

Complete the sentences below.

Put a cross [×] in the correct box for each question.

(a) Rachid lives in …

☐	**A** the north of France.
☐	**B** a big town.
☐	**C** the centre of France.

(b) He thinks that the streets are …

☐	**A** noisy.
☐	**B** crowded.
☐	**C** clean.

(c) He complains that when there are festivals …

☐	**A** there is too much noise.
☐	**B** there is a lot of pollution.
☐	**C** there are no good future prospects.

(3 marks)

Had a go ☐ Nearly there ☐ Nailed it! ☐

Local environment and transport

My area in the past

Where I live

1 Clara is talking about her area.

What does she say?

Listen to the recording and complete the sentences by putting a cross [×] in the correct box for each question.

(a) In Clara's village there ...

☐	**A** are no shops.
☐	**B** is one shop.
☐	**C** is only one person she knows.

(b) The nearest town is ...

☐	**A** 5 kilometres away.
☐	**B** 5 minutes away.
☐	**C** very small.

(c) Clara used to live ...

☐	**A** with her friends.
☐	**B** in the town.
☐	**C** in a house.

(3 marks)

My town, now and in the past

2 Ahmed has written a blog about his town.

> Quand j'avais cinq ans, ma ville, qui est située dans le sud-ouest de la France, était moins propre et il y avait beaucoup de bouteilles jetées dans les rues. Heureusement, on a essayé d'améliorer ma région et maintenant, j'aime bien le centre-ville où on peut marcher sans avoir peur, car au passé, il y avait plus de crime et de violence.
> Je vis au bord de la mer et la plage est excellente, mais il y a dix ans, il y avait trop de pollution.

Answer the following questions **in English**. There is no need to answer in complete sentences.

(a) What was Ahmed's town like when he was five years old? Give **two** details.

.... **(2 marks)**

(b) Why does Ahmed like the town centre nowadays?

.... **(1 mark)**

(c) What does Ahmed say about the seaside ten years ago?

.... **(1 mark)**

Tourism

Had a go ☐ Nearly there ☐ Nailed it! ☐

Town or country

Living in the countryside

1 Lola, Mohamed and Sarah are talking about the advantages and disadvantages of living in the countryside.

What do they say?

Listen to the podcast and complete the following tables **in English**.

You do not need to write in full sentences.

(a) Lola

Advantage:	
Disadvantage:	

(b) Mohamed

Advantage:	
Disadvantage:	

(c) Sarah

Advantage:	
Disadvantage:	

(6 marks)

Picture-based task: Countryside

See this photo in colour

2 Describe the picture. Write four short sentences **in French**.

....

....

....

.... **(8 marks)**

40

Had a go ☐ Nearly there ☐ Nailed it! ☐   Tourism

During the holidays

My holiday

1 Luis has written a diary entry about his holiday.

> Hier, c'était vraiment génial, car mes copains et moi sommes allés au bord de la mer où nous avons joué au football sur la plage avant de prendre le car pour aller en ville. Après avoir mangé un repas excellent, nous sommes rentrés à l'hôtel, fatigués mais heureux. Cet après-midi, je vais passer la journée chez des amis de mes parents qui habitent dans une très grande maison tout près de la plage et on va bien s'amuser.

What does he say?

Put a cross [×] next to each one of the **three** correct statements.

☐	A	Luis enjoyed his activities yesterday.
☐	B	Luis travelled to town by coach.
☐	C	Luis and his friends ate at the hotel.
☐	D	Luis was tired but sad at the end of the day.
☐	E	Luis is going to make a long journey this afternoon.
☐	F	Luis is going to spend the day with friends of his parents.

(3 marks)

> Be careful of 'false friends' (words which look like English words but which mean something different) such as *journée* ('day') or *car* ('coach')!

Translation

2 Translate the following passage **into French**.

> Last year I went to Martinique with my family. I spent hours on the beach where I played football and I watched the boats. It was sunny, so we were outside the whole time. I like going abroad because I love to discover different cultures and to try new meals. Next year, in July, we are going to visit Canada.

> Make sure that you have the correct word for 'to spend' as it's time not money!

....
....
....
....
....
....
....

(10 marks)

Tourism

Had a go ☐   Nearly there ☐   Nailed it! ☐

Abroad

Spending time abroad

1 Read these comments from an internet forum.

> **Mathis:** Je vais visiter ma famille en Afrique cette année. Je vais voyager en avion avec mes parents.
>
> **Fatima:** Le mois dernier je suis allée à l'étranger, chez mon oncle et ma tante. Nous avons passé deux semaines à Madagascar, une grande île d'Afrique.
>
> **Nathan:** Chaque année, je passe mes vacances en Amérique avec mon meilleur ami qui habite dans l'est du pays. Je passe un mois avec lui.

Who says what? Choose the correct answers.

Put a cross [×] in the correct column for each question.

	Who …	Mathis	Fatima	Nathan
(a)	… spends time with their best friend?			
(b)	… is going to visit Africa?			
(c)	… is going to travel by plane?			
(d)	… went on holiday for a fortnight?			
(e)	… goes to the same destination every year?			
(f)	… went on holiday last month?			

(6 marks)

> Take care with *mois* ('month') and *Afrique* ('Africa') as they appear in two different people's comments.

Writing about holidays

2 Write about holidays for an online magazine.

You **must** include the following points:

- why holidays are important
- your favourite place to visit
- what happened on a recent holiday
- your holiday plans for next year.

> Don't worry if you don't have experiences to answer a question truthfully. Invent something to show the French you know.

Write your answer **in French**. You should aim to write between 130 and 150 words.

....

....

....

....

....

....

....

....

(22 marks)

Had a go ☐ Nearly there ☐ Nailed it! ☐   **Tourism**

Types of holiday

Picture-based task: Holidays

See this photo in colour

1 Describe the picture. Write four short sentences **in French**.

....

....

....

.... **(8 marks)**

Promoting Villeneuve

2 Listen to this advert promoting Villeneuve.

What is mentioned?

Listen to the recording and put a cross [×] in each one of the **three** correct boxes.

☐	A	sports
☐	B	shops
☐	C	beach
☐	D	transport
☐	E	weather
☐	F	places to eat

(3 marks)

Tourism

Had a go ☐ Nearly there ☐ Nailed it! ☐

Where to stay

Hotel advertisement

1 Read this advertisement.

> Petit hôtel au bord de la mer, près de la plage. Vingt-cinq chambres, piscine et jardin avec un café où on peut manger toute la journée!
> Repas excellent le soir au restaurant; petit-déjeuner et service inclus mais pas de déjeuner.
> Chiens acceptés.

Put a cross [×] in each one of the **three** correct boxes.

The hotel …

☐	A	is near the beach.
☐	B	has 35 rooms.
☐	C	has a swimming pool and a gym.
☐	D	serves an excellent lunch.
☐	E	includes breakfast and service in the price.
☐	F	accepts dogs.

(3 marks)

> Make sure you put a cross in the number of boxes required to fully answer the question. Here you need to choose three answers.

Read aloud

2 Lucas has contributed to a blog about where to stay on holiday. Read out the text below, then listen to the recording in the Answer section to check your pronunciation. **(8 marks)**

> Quand je pars en vacances, je passe souvent du temps dans un camping en France.
> Ma famille adore la nature et on aime bien dormir sous une tente.
> S'il fait froid, nous avons toujours quelques couvertures disponibles.
> Mes amis préfèrent un logement plus confortable comme un appartement ou un hôtel.

Listen to the recording

Follow-on questions

Once you have read the text aloud, listen to two questions related to what you have read.

You are expected to say a few words or a short phrase / sentence in response to each question. One-word answers will not be sufficient to gain full marks.

(4 marks)

Had a go ☐ Nearly there ☐ Nailed it! ☐   Tourism

Booking accommodation

Role play

1 **Setting: At a campsite**

   Scenario:
   - You are at a campsite in France.
   - Listen to the recording of the teacher's part.
   - The teacher will play the part of an employee at the campsite and will speak first.
   - Your teacher will ask questions **in French** and you must answer **in French**.
   - You are expected to say a few words or a short phrase / sentence in response to each prompt. One-word answers will not be sufficient to gain full marks.

   Task:
   1 Say how long you would like to stay.
   2 Say who is with you.
   3 Say what you want to visit.
   4 Say why you like camping.
   5 Ask a question about transport.

   (10 marks)

   In the Speaking exam you will be given time to prepare for the tasks. Make sure you keep your answers simple and try to speak clearly and confidently.

Booking a place to stay

2 Fatima is booking accommodation on the phone. What does she say?

   Complete the gap in each sentence using a word or phrase from the box below. There are more words / phrases than gaps.

on 6th April	on 16th February	on 16th April
on the 13th floor	on the 3rd floor	on the 2nd floor
a problem	a deposit to pay	a lift
an allergy	a dog	a wheelchair
10.00 pm	8.00 pm	the weekend

   (a) Fatima wants to book two rooms ....
   (b) She is offered rooms ....
   (c) She asks if there is ....
   (d) Her father has ....
   (e) Fatima will arrive at ....

   (5 marks)

Tourism — Had a go ☐   Nearly there ☐   Nailed it! ☐

Holiday activities

Writing about holiday activities

1 Write to your friend about holiday activities.

You **must** include the following points:
- what activities you do on holiday
- your favourite holiday activity and why you prefer it
- what you did on a recent holiday
- your plans for future activities on holiday.

Write your answer **in French**. You should aim to write between 80 and 90 words.

....
....
....
....
....
....
....
.... **(18 marks)**

Picture-based task: Sports activities

See this photo in colour

2 Describe the picture.

Your description **must** cover:
- people
- location
- activity. **(8 marks)**

Listen to the recording

Follow-on questions

When you have finished your description, listen to the recording of two questions relating to the picture. You are expected to say a few words or a short phrase / sentence in response to each question. One-word answers will not be sufficient to gain full marks.

(4 marks)

You can listen to sample answers in the Answer section.

Had a go ☐ Nearly there ☐ Nailed it! ☐   **Tourism**

Trips and excursions

Target grade 1-5

Translation

1 Translate the following sentences **into English**.

(a) J'adore visiter des villes historiques.

....

(b) La nature m'intéresse beaucoup.

....

(c) Je veux voyager à l'étranger avec ma famille.

....

(d) La semaine dernière, je suis allé à un beau village.

....

(e) Mon petit frère aime la vue du pont.

....

(10 marks)

> In translations, read through each sentence in full before trying to translate any of the words. It will give you a better sense of the meaning.

Target grade 7

A day out

2 Lucy is talking about an excursion. What does she say?

Listen to the recording and complete the sentences by putting a cross [×] in the correct box for each question.

(a) Lucy visited ...

☐	**A** an island.
☐	**B** a bridge.
☐	**C** a café.

(b) She used technology to help her to …

☐	**A** find her aunt's house.
☐	**B** locate the best restaurants.
☐	**C** find the best beach.

(c) Lucy visited ...

☐	**A** a market.
☐	**B** an interesting souvenir shop.
☐	**C** a clothes shop.

(d) Her trip lasted ...

☐	**A** 4 days.
☐	**B** 2 days.
☐	**C** 4 hours.

(4 marks)

47

Tourism

Had a go ☐   Nearly there ☐   Nailed it! ☐

Asking for help or directions

Role play

1 **Setting: At a campsite**

   Scenario:

   • You are in a campsite in Switzerland, and you are reporting a problem.
   • Listen to the recording of the teacher's part.
   • The teacher will play the part of the receptionist and will speak first.
   • Your teacher will ask questions **in French** and you must answer **in French** in the pauses. If you need more time, pause the recording.
   • You are expected to say a few words or a short phrase / sentence in response to each prompt. One-word answers will not be sufficient to gain full marks.

   > **Task:**
   > 1 Describe the problem with the campsite.
   > 2 Say what your name is.
   > 3 Say how many nights you are staying for.
   > 4 Give your opinion of the campsite you are staying in.
   > 5 Ask a question about directions to town.

   (10 marks)

   > To report a problem, you might want to use a negative phrase, so remember that *ne ... pas* will sit around the verb.

Asking for directions

2 Clément is talking about asking for help.

   Listen to the recording and complete the sentences by putting a cross [×] in the correct box for each question.

   (a) Yesterday Clément had help from ...

☐	**A** a woman.
☐	**B** a man.
☐	**C** a girl.

   (b) He was accompanied to the ...

☐	**A** river.
☐	**B** tourist office.
☐	**C** flat.

   (c) Clément lost ...

☐	**A** money.
☐	**B** his shoe.
☐	**C** his friend.

   (3 marks)

48

Had a go ☐   Nearly there ☐   Nailed it! ☐   Tourism

Shopping for gifts

Role play

1 Setting: **In a gift shop**

   Scenario:
   - You are in a gift shop in France.
   - Listen to the recording of the teacher's part.
   - The teacher will play the part of the shop assistant and will speak first.
   - The teacher will ask questions **in French** and you must answer **in French**.
   - You are expected to say a few words or a short phrase / sentence in response to each prompt. One-word answers will not be sufficient to gain full marks.

   > **Task:**
   > 1 Say what gift you want to buy.
   > 2 Say who you are buying the gift for.
   > 3 Say why you are buying the gift.
   > 4 Give your opinion of the item you have been shown.
   > 5 Ask about the price.

   (10 marks)

   > You can use the same construction (for example *c'est*) more than once as long as you communicate clearly.

Buying presents

2 Louis is talking about buying presents.

   What does he say?

   Put a cross [×] next to each one of the **two** correct statements.

☐	A	Louis finds it hard to buy presents for all his family.
☐	B	Louis's father hates clothes.
☐	C	Louis's father likes reading.
☐	D	Louis has just bought a gift for his brother.

   (2 marks)

Tourism

Had a go ☐ Nearly there ☐ Nailed it! ☐

Tourist information

Tourist information

1 You find this tourist brochure in a tourist information office in France.

> La vieille ville est populaire avec les touristes, car on peut y visiter beaucoup de bâtiments historiques. La grande tour à deux kilomètres de la ville sera ouverte au public en août. La vue est excellente et on pourra y trouver un petit musée sur la nature.
> On accueille les touristes avec un plan de la ville gratuit et on peut aussi réserver une visite du parc qui se trouve juste à côté de la tour. Ce n'est pas cher. On peut toujours trouver une table au café, où les repas sont *incroyables*; les gâteaux sont particulièrement délicieux!
> Si vous voulez d'autres renseignements, téléphonez-nous.

Complete the sentences below.

Put a cross [×] in the correct box for each question.

(a) The old town is popular with tourists because of …

☐	A the tours offered.
☐	B the historic buildings.
☐	C the pleasant walks.

(b) The tall tower will …

☐	A be open in August.
☐	B attract wildlife.
☐	C not interest young people.

(c) Tourists receive …

☐	A a free meal.
☐	B a free town map.
☐	C a free excursion.

(d) Which of these is the best translation for the word *incroyables*?

☐	A fully booked
☐	B disgusting
☐	C unbelievable

(4 marks)

Read aloud

2 Sarah, your friend from Belgium, has sent you some information about tourism in her area. Read out the text below.

> J'habite en ville.
> On peut visiter un musée et un pont.
> Il y a beaucoup de touristes en été.
> Le grand château est très intéressant.
> J'aime faire les magasins dans le centre avec mes amis.

(8 marks)

> The *i* of *ville* is pronounced as an ee sound.

> Remember that in French lots of consonants are silent at the end of the word. For example *peut, pont, intéressant* all have a silent final t and *magasins* and *amis* have a silent final s.

> Where a final consonant is followed by a vowel, you **usually** pronounce it. This is called **liaison**. Here, there is liaison of the final **s** in *très* in *très intéressant*.

50

Had a go ☐   Nearly there ☐   Nailed it! ☐   **Tourism**

Tourist attractions

Picture-based task

See this photo in colour

1 Describe the picture. Write four short sentences **in French**.

   ....

   ....

   ....

   .... **(8 marks)**

Tourist attractions

2 Ahmed, Myriam and Clément are talking about tourist attractions.

   What do they say?

   Listen to the recording and complete the sentences by putting a cross [×] in the correct box for each question.

   (a) Ahmed saw lots of ...

☐	**A** museums.
☐	**B** paintings.
☐	**C** buildings.

   (b) Myriam ...

☐	**A** has been to the mountains.
☐	**B** does not like being active.
☐	**C** is going to try some winter sports.

   (c) Clément likes tourist attractions which ...

☐	**A** are historic.
☐	**B** are near rivers.
☐	**C** his parents like.

   (3 marks)

Tourism

Had a go ☐ Nearly there ☐ Nailed it! ☐

Holiday problems

Problems on holiday

1 Marie writes in her diary.

> Je n'aime pas aller en vacances à l'étranger car il y a toujours des problèmes et je ne dors jamais bien. Souvent, je déteste ce qu'on mange aux repas, et il fait toujours trop chaud!. L'année dernière au Canada, j'ai laissé mon portable dans un café, mais mon frère l'a trouvé. Je préfère rester chez moi et sortir avec mes amis dans ma propre région.

Put a cross [×] in each one of the **three** correct boxes.

☐ A	Marie likes going on holiday abroad.
☐ B	Marie hates meals on holiday.
☐ C	Marie likes the warm weather abroad.
☐ D	Last year she went to Canada.
☐ E	Her brother lost his money in a café.
☐ F	Someone found her mobile phone.

(3 marks)

> Make sure that if more than one person is mentioned in a text, you have the right person for an action or activity.

A difficult trip

2 You hear Toni talking about holiday problems on a French radio programme.

What does she say?

Answer the following questions **in English**.

You do not need to write in full sentences.

(a) How did Toni and her aunt travel?

.... **(1 mark)**

(b) When did they arrive at the hotel?

.... **(1 mark)**

(c) What two problems happened on the first day?

.... **(2 marks)**

(d) What happened after Toni and her aunt had their meal? (Give **two** details.)

.... **(2 marks)**

Had a go ☐ Nearly there ☐ Nailed it! ☐   **Tourism**

Accommodation problems

Problems with accommodation

1 Read this article about accommodation problems which Sacha has written.

> D'habitude, j'adore aller en vacances car je m'amuse bien avec ma famille. Par contre, je viens de rentrer de vacances vraiment nulles dans un hôtel en France. D'abord, il n'y avait pas d'ascenseur et notre chambre était au cinquième étage! J'ai trouvé les repas assez bons, mais il y avait trop de bruit le soir et je n'ai pas bien dormi. Le dernier jour des vacances, on a volé la valise de ma mère et on a dû appeler la police. Mes parents vont écrire au patron de l'hôtel pour lui expliquer les problèmes qu'on a eu. Je pense que nous n'irons plus à cet hôtel!

Put a cross [×] in each one of the **three** correct boxes.

☐	A	Sacha has just returned from a holiday.
☐	B	There was no lift in the hotel.
☐	C	Sacha disliked the meals in the hotel.
☐	D	She slept quite well.
☐	E	Sacha's mother was arrested by the police.
☐	F	Someone stole a suitcase.

(3 marks)

> Look at the text carefully and read it through first before you start to answer the questions as it's important to be sure of the general meaning of the passage.

Translation

2 Translate the paragraph **into French**.

> I like going on holiday, but there are often accommodation problems. In July, I spent a week in a bad hotel with my favourite uncle. My room was not clean and there was too much noise in the restaurant in the evenings. There was also no lift. Next year, I would like to go camping.

....
....
....
....
....
....
....

(10 marks)

> There won't be a word for **in** when you translate 'in the evenings'.

> 'To go camping' won't be translated with *aller*!

Tourism

Had a go ☐ Nearly there ☐ Nailed it! ☐

Eating out

A restaurant review

1. Write a review of a restaurant for a website.

   You **must** include the following points:
   - what meals they serve
   - your opinion of the restaurant
   - when you will next visit the restaurant.

   Write your answer **in French**. You should aim to write between 40 and 50 words.

   ....
   ....
   ....
   ....
   ....
   ....
   ....

   (14 marks)

> Don't worry if you can't remember a specific word, try and find other ways to say the same thing. Here, if you don't know 'to serve', you could write *Sur le menu, il y a …* or *On peut manger …* .

Role play

2. **Setting: In a restaurant**

   Scenario:
   - You are in a restaurant in France with a friend.
   - Listen to the recording of the teacher's part.
   - The teacher will play the part of the employee and will speak first.
   - The teacher will ask questions **in French** and you must answer **in French**.
   - You are expected to say a few words or a short phrase / sentence in response to each prompt. One-word answers will not be sufficient to gain full marks.

   Listen to the recording

   Task:
   1. Say what you would like to eat.
   2. Ask the price of something on the menu.
   3. Say what your favourite drink is.
   4. Say what you will eat tomorrow.
   5. Ask a question about opening times of the restaurant.

   > If you don't know the name of your favourite drink in French, just name any drink that you do know.

   (10 marks)

Had a go ☐ **Nearly there** ☐ **Nailed it!** ☐   Tourism

Opinions about food

Eating out

1 Toni is talking about food.

> Hier, ma famille est allée à un nouveau restaurant qui est situé dans un petit village. J'ai trouvé la cuisine nulle. Comme entrée, j'ai choisi des pâtes, mais elles n'étaient pas savoureuses. Après avoir fini, j'ai essayé le poisson avec les frites et c'était assez agréable, mais les fruits que j'ai pris en dessert étaient très aigres. Mon frère a choisi une glace qu'il a trouvé excellente.

What does Toni say about the food?

Put a cross [×] next to each one of the **three** correct statements.

☐	A	Toni went to a restaurant in a small town.
☐	B	She found the starter tasty.
☐	C	She quite liked the fish and chips she ate.
☐	D	She had an ice cream.
☐	E	She found the fruit sour.
☐	F	Her brother enjoyed his dessert.

(3 marks)

> Remember to check how many answers you need to select. Here you need to choose three.

Dictation

2 You are going to hear someone talking about food.

Sentences 1–3: write down the missing words in the gaps provided. In each gap, you will write one word **in French**.

1 Mon père .... les ....

2 Je ne .... pas de ....

3 Ma .... adore les ....

Sentences 4–6: write down the full sentences that you hear in the spaces provided, **in French**.

4 ....

5 ....

6 ....

(10 marks)

Tourism

Had a go ☐   Nearly there ☐   Nailed it! ☐

The weather

Translation

1 Translate the following five sentences **into French**.

(a) I like hot weather.

....

(b) I go to the beach at the weekend.

....

(c) When it's bad weather I stay at home.

....

(d) Last week it snowed every day.

....

(e) If it's cold weather, I'm sad.

....

> In French you would translate this as 'I like when it is hot' but as long as your translation conveys the message you will be credited.

> 'it's bad weather' = *il fait mauvais*.

> You need to say 'all the days' here.

(10 marks)

Today's weather

2 You hear this weather report on the radio.

What does it say?

Complete the sentences by putting a cross [×] in the correct box for each question.

(a) This afternoon in the south the weather will be ...

☐	**A** hot.
☐	**B** colder.
☐	**C** windy.

(b) It will be foggy all day in ...

☐	**A** the north.
☐	**B** the mountains.
☐	**C** the west.

(c) Tomorrow in the east ...

☐	**A** the sky will be blue.
☐	**B** it will rain.
☐	**C** it will be cold.

(3 marks)

Had a go ☐ Nearly there ☐ Nailed it! ☐   **Tourism**

Customs and festivals

Role play

1 Setting: **At the tourist information office**

Scenario:
- You are at a tourist information office in France.
- Listen to the recording of the teacher's part.
- The teacher will play the part of an employee at the tourist information office and will speak first.
- The teacher will ask questions **in French** and you must answer **in French**.
- You are expected to say a few words or a short phrase / sentence in response to each prompt. One-word answers will not be sufficient to gain full marks.

> **Task:**
> 1 Say what event you want to visit.
> 2 Say how long you are staying.
> 3 Say what you will do tomorrow.
> 4 Ask a question about local festivals.
> 5 Ask for a recommendation for a hotel.

(10 marks)

> If you don't know a particular word, try thinking of words that you do know to say a similar thing. For example, here if you don't know 'local', you could say 'festivals in the region'.

> In the Speaking exam, your teacher will address you using the formal *vous* but it is fine for you to respond using the informal *tu*.

Translation

2 Translate the following five sentences **into French**.

(a) I love festivals.

....

(b) I like cultural events in my town.

....

(c) My French friend finds concerts interesting.

....

(d) Last week I went to a party with my friends.

....

(e) I want to visit Paris on 14 July.

....

(10 marks)

> There is no word for 'on' in sentence (e).

57

Tourism

Had a go ☐ Nearly there ☐ Nailed it! ☐

Visiting a city

A town I visited

1 As part of a conversation topic, you might talk about a recent visit to a place. Prepare answers to this question and then speak for about 30 seconds about it.

> As part of a conversation, you need to answer this question as fully as you can.

(a) Parle-moi d'une visite récente dans une grande ville.

Describing a town

See this photo in colour

2 Describe the picture.

Your description **must** cover:
- people
- location
- activity.

(8 marks)

Listen to the recording

Follow-on questions

When you have finished your description, listen to the recording of two questions relating to the picture. You are expected to say a few words or a short phrase / sentence in response to each question. One-word answers will not be sufficient to gain full marks.

(4 marks)

Had a go ☐   Nearly there ☐   Nailed it! ☐   **My school**

School subjects

My school life

1 Thomas is talking about school life.

What does he say?

Complete the gap in each sentence using a word or phrase from the box below.

There are more words / phrases than gaps.

> history   science   art
> technology   media   sport

(a) Thomas studies .... and .... **(2 marks)**

(b) Next year he is going to study .... **(1 mark)**

> So many school subjects are mentioned that you will really need to listen carefully for specific details. In question (b) listen for a time phrase which will point you to the future.

Who studies which subjects?

2 Read these comments from an internet forum.

Eva:	Dans ma classe de maths, il y a trop d'élèves. Je n'aime pas cette matière.
Enzo:	Je n'étudie pas le théâtre mais j'ai des cours de technologie.
Maxime:	J'étudie les langues et l'art. Je vais continuer d'étudier le théâtre plus tard.

> Look carefully at any negative phrases, don't just look for the subjects.

Who says what? Choose the correct answers.

Put a cross [×] in the correct column for each question.

	Who ...	Eva	Enzo	Maxime
(a)	... will study drama?			
(b)	... studies technology?			
(c)	... doesn't study drama?			
(d)	... studies languages?			
(e)	... has a crowded class?			
(f)	... dislikes Maths?			

(6 marks)

My school   Had a go ☐   Nearly there ☐   Nailed it! ☐

School likes, dislikes and reasons

My school

1   Rachid has written an email about his school.

> Au collège, j'étudie l'anglais, mais je trouve ça assez dur et mon prof est trop sévère. Cependant, puisque la lecture m'intéresse beaucoup, j'adore le français. Selon moi, les maths, c'est nul.
>
> Hier, pendant un cours de sciences, je n'ai pas compris ce que ma prof a dit mais elle a refusé d'expliquer. Je n'étais pas content ! Demain, il y aura une épreuve de technologie et je dois améliorer mes compétences car je voudrais avoir de bonnes notes.

Answer the following questions **in English**. You do not need to write in full sentences.

(a) What does Rachid think of English? ....

(b) Why does he like French? ....

(c) What did Rachid's teacher refuse to do yesterday? ....

(d) What has Rachid got tomorrow? ....

(e) Why will he need to improve his skills? ....

(5 marks)

Read aloud

2   Zoé, your friend from France, has sent you some information about her school.

Read out the text below.

> J'étudie neuf matières.
> Je préfère l'anglais et les maths.
> Je trouve l'histoire très intéressante.
> Je n'aime pas le sport car c'est fatigant.
> Mon prof de science donne trop de devoirs.

(8 marks)

Listen to the recording to practise some of these sounds:
j, je
r, trouve
è, très
é, intéressant
très intéressante

Track 47

Follow-on questions

Once you have read the text aloud, answer these two questions related to what you have read.

You are expected to say a few words or a short phrase / sentence in response to each question.

One-word answers will not be sufficient to gain full marks.

(a) Qu'est-ce que tu préfères comme matières?

(b) Qu'est-ce que tu penses des devoirs?

(4 marks)

Had a go ☐   Nearly there ☐   Nailed it! ☐   **My school**

Timetable and school day

Translation

1 Translate the following five sentences **into French**.

> In French, the word 'the' is always included before school subjects, for example *l'anglais, les maths*.

(a) I like going to school.

....

(b) My favourite subject is English.

....

(c) My brother hates Maths because he finds it very difficult.

....

(d) Last year I had lots of homework.

....

(e) If I get good marks, I can continue my education.

.... **(10 marks)**

Different schools

2 Emma and Nathan are talking about their schools.

What do they say?

Listen to the recording and complete the sentences by putting a cross [×] in the correct box for each question.

(a) Emma thinks her school …

☐	A starts too early.
☐	B starts too late.
☐	C serves good food.

(b) At lunchtime she …

☐	A goes home.
☐	B is really hungry.
☐	C is tired.

(c) Nathan's journey to school …

☐	A is pleasant.
☐	B is often noisy.
☐	C is by car.

(d) His friends …

☐	A know the route.
☐	B are never on time.
☐	C try to do homework whilst travelling.

(4 marks)

My school — Had a go ☐ Nearly there ☐ Nailed it! ☐

Equipment and facilities in school

Describing school

1 Write to your friend about school.

You **must** include the following points:
- a description of your school
- your opinion of your school with reasons
- how you went to school last week
- your future plans for studying.

Write your answer **in French**. You should aim to write between 80 and 90 words.

....
....
....
....
....
....
....
....
....
....
....
....
....

(18 marks)

> Make sure you address all four bullet points in your answer and try to develop your responses as much as you can.

My school life

2 Hugo is talking about schools in a podcast.

What does he say?

Complete the gap in each sentence using a word or phrase from the box below.

There are more words / phrases than gaps.

> excellent   interesting   useful   difficult
> IT room   library   classrooms   office
> field   dining hall   sports hall   gymnasium

(a) Hugo finds studying media ....

(b) He does research in the ....

(c) The only place he can do sport is in the ....

(3 marks)

Had a go ☐   Nearly there ☐   Nailed it! ☐   **My school**

School uniform

Opinion on school uniform

1   Read this email written by Mathis.

> ✉
>
> Dans mon école, je dois porter un uniforme scolaire qui n'est pas à la mode. Le pantalon est marron et la veste est bleue. Je suis pour l'uniforme car ça cache les différences entre les riches et les pauvres et aussi, l'uniforme peut encourager les élèves à bien se comporter. Cependant, il faut changer les couleurs et j'espère qu'on pourra bientôt porter des vêtements plus confortables.

Answer the following questions **in English**. There is no need to answer in full sentences.

(a) Why does Mathis object to his uniform?

....   **(1 mark)**

(b) Give two reasons why Mathis supports school uniform.

....   **(2 marks)**

(c) What does Mathis say must happen?

....   **(1 mark)**

(d) What would he like to be able to wear?

....   **(1 mark)**

> The phrase *il faut* ... expresses that something is necessary.

My school uniform

2   Emma is talking about school uniform.

What does she mention?

Listen to the recording and put a cross [×] in each one of the **three** correct boxes.

☐	**A** jumper
☐	**B** shirt
☐	**C** socks
☐	**D** tie
☐	**E** skirt
☐	**F** shoes

(3 marks)

> The French words for 'shoes' and 'socks' are quite similar, so pay attention!

My school

Had a go ☐ Nearly there ☐ Nailed it! ☐

Class activities

A school show

1 You see this poster in a French school about a show.

> **Samedi dix mai**
>
> Venez voir le spectacle de notre classe d'anglais dans la salle de classe 12 à la pause-déjeuner.
>
> Entrée: 2 euros

What things are mentioned?

Put a cross [×] in each one of the **three** correct boxes.

☐	A	the date of the show
☐	B	what the show is called
☐	C	where the show is taking place
☐	D	the entry cost
☐	E	what food to bring
☐	F	the exact time of the show

(3 marks)

> Pay attention to how many answers are required. Here you need to select three options.

A school exchange

2 Mohamed is talking about a visit.

Listen to the recording and answer the following questions **in English**. There is no need to answer in full sentences.

Listen to the recording

(a) Who told Mohamed about the exchange?

.... **(1 mark)**

(b) Why is Mohamed stressed?

.... **(1 mark)**

(c) What two advantages of an exchange does Mohamed mention?

.... **(2 marks)**

(d) What does he hope will happen?

.... **(1 mark)**

> Listen carefully for each detail. If you hear one answer that you are sure of, it might help you to locate the answer to another question, as the answers come in order.

Had a go ☐ **Nearly there** ☐ **Nailed it!** ☐

My school

School rules

Talking about school rules

1. Answer these questions as part of a longer conversation about school life.

   (a) Qu'est-ce que tu penses des règles scolaires?

   (b) Comment est-ce que tu changerais les règles scolaires?

   (c) Est-ce que tu es pour ou contre l'uniforme scolaire?

> Try to use at least one other time frame as well as the present tense, even when the question may be asked in a specific tense.

> You will often be asked for an opinion. Revise ways to introduce your opinion and adjectives to help you to say what you think. Here are just some, but there are many more you should know.
>
> | | |
> |---|---|
> | *selon moi, …* – in my opinion, … | *ennuyeux* – boring |
> | *à mon avis, …* – in my opinion, … | *confortable* – comfortable |
> | *je pense que …* – I think that … | *difficile* – difficult |
> | *je suis d'accord avec …* – I agree with … | *intéressant* – interesting |
> | *Ça m'est égal.* – I don't mind. | *excellent* – excellent |
> | *je suis contre …* – I am against … | *extraordinaire* – extraordinary |
> | *je suis pour …* – I am for … | *juste* – fair |
> | | *important* – important |
> | | *nécessaire* – necessary, essential |
> | | *possible* – possible |
> | | *utile* – useful |

(H ONLY)

My school's rules

2. Jules is talking about his school's rules.

   Answer the following questions **in English**. There is no need to answer in full sentences.

   (a) What does Jules think about the rules at his school?

   .... **(1 mark)**

   (b) What happened to his friend last week?

   .... **(2 marks)**

   (c) How does Jules describe his school uniform?

   .... **(2 marks)**

   (d) What does he think about having to wear a school uniform?

   .... **(1 mark)**

> Listen carefully for each detail. If you hear one answer that you are sure of, it might help you to locate the answer to another question, as the answers come in order.

My school — Had a go ☐ Nearly there ☐ Nailed it! ☐

Opinions about school

My opinion of school

1. Write about your school for an online magazine.

   You **must** include the following points:
   - why your school is a good or bad school
   - your opinion of teachers
   - a recent school event
   - your education plans for next year.

   Write your answer **in French**. You should aim to write between 130 and 150 words.

   ....

   ....

   ....

   ....

   ....

   ....

   ....

   ....

   ....

   ....

   ....

   ....

   ....

   .... **(22 marks)**

At school

2. Fatima is talking about her school.

   What does she mention?

   Listen to the recording and put a cross [×] in each one of the **three** correct boxes.

☐	A	timetable
☐	B	teachers
☐	C	meals
☐	D	school subjects
☐	E	buildings
☐	F	homework

   (3 marks)

Had a go ☐ **Nearly there** ☐ **Nailed it!** ☐   My school

Clubs and activities

Translation

1 Translate the paragraph **into French**.

> I like going to clubs at school. My favourite activity is athletics. I often run with my friends on Thursdays after finishing lessons. Last month we took part in a sporting competition, and I won. In the future I'd really like to try to learn a musical instrument because it's fun.

....

....

....

....

....

....

....

....

.... **(10 marks)**

Although *activité* is feminine, 'my' will be *mon* here because it is **before a vowel**.

'Often' will come after 'run'.   There's no word for 'on' before 'Thursdays'.

'After finishing' needs to be translated by 'after having finished'.

Translation

2 Translate the following sentences **into English**.

(a) J'aime les clubs à l'école.

....

(b) Mes amis ont cours de cuisine le lundi.

....

(c) Je déteste le théâtre car c'est difficile.

....

(d) La semaine dernière, j'ai joué au foot après le dernier cours.

....

(e) Je vais me reposer.

.... **(10 marks)**

| My school | Had a go ☐ Nearly there ☐ Nailed it! ☐ |

Success at school

Your school successes

1 As part of a conversation topic, you might talk about what you do well at school. Prepare your answer to this question, then speak for about 30 seconds about it.

(a) Qu'est-ce que tu as réussi au collège?

> You might be asked a question like this in the conversation part of your Speaking exam. Don't panic, but think of the vocabulary you know in relation to success in school. That could be passing exams, playing sport, winning a competition, learning a language, improving your maths, doing your homework every day – choose something you know the French for and remember it doesn't have to be the truth! It is an opportunity to show off what you know.

Exams diary entry

2 Alessandro has written this diary entry.

> Je suis stressé car je ne sais pas si je réussirai mes examens à la fin de cette année. J'ai essayé d'améliorer mes compétences en langues et en histoire, car je ne suis pas fort en anglais et je trouve l'histoire vraiment dure. Je crois que mes efforts vont m'aider.

Complete the sentences below.

Put a cross [×] in the correct box for each question.

(a) Alessandro is stressed because …

☐	**A** he has not worked hard.
☐	**B** he doesn't know if he will pass his exams.
☐	**C** he finds exams very difficult.

(b) He has tried to …

☐	**A** ask for help.
☐	**B** improve his skills in languages.
☐	**C** look at the history of languages.

(c) He finds history …

☐	**A** easy.
☐	**B** useful.
☐	**C** hard.

(3 marks)

Had a go ☐ Nearly there ☐ Nailed it! ☐ **My school**

Options at 16

Your future plans

1 As part of a conversation topic, you might talk about what you are going to do next year. Prepare your answer to this question, then speak for about 30 seconds about it.

(a) Qu'est-ce que tu vas choisir d'étudier l'année prochaine?

> The question is about the future, so you need to answer with a future time frame but you can include other tenses as well – what you have thought about, what you have already done or are doing to prepare for next year.

My post-16 options

2 Read Charlie's message on a discussion forum.

> Je m'appelle Charlie et je viens d'avoir quinze ans. En septembre, je dois choisir ce que je veux faire après mes examens.
>
> Mon ami veut aller au lycée, et aller ensuite à l'université. Moi, je ne suis pas sûr. Je suis assez créatif donc je pense que je voudrais faire quelque chose de pratique. Je vais probablement faire une formation dans une entreprise locale qui organise des fêtes.
>
> Je vais discuter de mes choix avec mes parents. Ma mère pense que je dois devenir *instituteur* mais je ne veux pas retourner à l'école et je n'aime pas beaucoup les enfants!

Complete the sentences below. Put a cross [×] in the correct box for each question.

(a) Charlie has just turned …

☐	**A** 14.
☐	**B** 15.
☐	**C** 16.

(b) Next year, Charlie's friend wants to …

☐	**A** go to sixth form college.
☐	**B** go to university.
☐	**C** do his exams.

(c) Charlie wants to…

☐	**A** be sure.
☐	**B** choose something different.
☐	**C** do something practical.

(d) He thinks he might …

☐	**A** do some training with a local company.
☐	**B** go to lots of parties.
☐	**C** stay with his parents.

(e) Which of these is the best translation for the word *instituteur*?
Put a cross [×] in the correct box.

☐	**A** primary school teacher
☐	**B** librarian
☐	**C** illustrator

(5 marks)

My future studies

3 Inès is in school and is discussing options with her teacher.

What does she say? Listen to the recording and complete the following table **in English**. You do not need to write in full sentences.

(a)	a subject she hates	………………………………………… .
(b)	her favourite subject	………………………………………… .
(c)	her final choice	………………………………………… .

(3 marks)

My school

Had a go ☐ Nearly there ☐ Nailed it! ☐

Schools – France and the UK

Comparing education systems

1 Prepare your answer to this question, then speak about it for about 30 seconds.

(a) Tu préfères le système d'éducation en France ou au Royaume-Uni? Pourquoi?

> You might be asked this question as part of the conversation task in your Speaking exam.

> You are being asked an opinion, so you can use the language you have learned to give opinions e.g. *je pense que, à mon avis, je trouve, je préfère*. You could also use a flexible phrase such as *C'est une question intéressante* as part of your answer.

Schools in France and the UK

2 Dorian has written a blog about schools in France and the UK.

> À mon avis, les écoles françaises commencent beaucoup trop tôt et le système d'éducation britannique est meilleur car les cours finissent entre trois heures et trois heures et demie. Je sais que nous avons plus de vacances en été, mais après un mois, je commence toujours à m'ennuyer. Je préférerais avoir une journée moins longue. Mes parents aussi préféreraient ne pas devoir acheter mes livres et mes cahiers car ils dépensent beaucoup d'argent pour ça.

What does Dorian say about the different school systems in France and the UK?

Put a cross [×] next to each one of the **three** correct statements.

☐	A	Dorian says that he prefers the French system of education.
☐	B	Dorian says that British schools have different finishing times.
☐	C	Dorian gets bored in the holidays.
☐	D	Dorian's parents don't agree with him.
☐	E	Dorian says that he'd prefer a longer day.
☐	F	Dorian's parents have to buy his books.

(3 marks)

> Make sure you read the whole passage through at least once before attempting the questions. When there are comparisons in a text, you need to ensure you are answering the correct part of the question and understanding the whole passage will help.

Had a go ☐ Nearly there ☐ Nailed it! ☐ **My future**

Future study plans

Picture-based task: University

See this photo in colour

> Normally, one of these questions will be in a past tense, but practise using a future time frame here.

1. Describe the picture.

   Your description must cover:
   - people
   - location
   - activity. **(8 marks)**

   Follow-on questions

   When you have finished your description, listen to the recording of two questions relating to your picture. You are expected to say a few words or a short phrase / sentence in response to each question. One-word answers will not be sufficient to gain full marks. **(4 marks)**

After leaving school

2. Read these comments from an internet forum.

   > **Mathis:** Je sais exactement ce que je vais faire après avoir quitté le lycée. Si c'est possible, j'étudierai dans une université en Angleterre car je voudrais améliorer mon anglais.
   >
   > **Sacha:** L'année prochaine, je quitterai l'école. Je voudrais faire une formation car je serai payée. Je ne voudrais pas aller à l'université dans le futur car ce sera trop cher.

   Complete the tables **in English**. You do not need to write in full sentences.

   (a) Mathis

His future education plans	
Reason why	

   (b) Sacha

Her future education plans	
Reason why	

   (4 marks)

My future

Had a go ☐ Nearly there ☐ Nailed it! ☐

Future plans

My future plans

1 Read Enzo's blog about his future plans.

> Je vais bientôt avoir seize ans et j'ai commencé à penser au futur. Je sais que je voudrais avoir deux chiens et que j'aimerais habiter dans une grande maison avec un jardin dans le sud de la France. Mais je veux aussi voyager dans les pays européens. Mon ambition est d'étudier à l'université et de devenir *ingénieur* car j'aime les maths, la science et la technologie.

Complete the sentences below.

Put a cross [×] in the correct box for each question.

(a) Enzo is …

☐ **A** 16.
☐ **B** 15.
☐ **C** 17.

(b) He would like to live …

☐ **A** in many European countries.
☐ **B** in the west of France.
☐ **C** in the south of France.

(c) He wants to have …

☐ **A** a big house and a garden.
☐ **B** three dogs.
☐ **C** a big house with a garage.

(d) What is the best translation of the word *ingénieur*?

☐ **A** engineer
☐ **B** illustrator
☐ **C** lawyer

(4 marks)

> There are clues of *maths*, *science* and *technologie* to help you work out the answer to (d).

My ideal job

2 Listen to Morgane talking about her future plans. Listen to the recording and answer the following questions **in English**.

You do not need to write in full sentences.

Listen to the recording

(a) What is Morgane's ideal job?

.... **(1 mark)**

(b) What two drawbacks to the job does she mention?

.... **(2 marks)**

(c) What does she say is important about holidays?

.... **(1 mark)**

(d) What does she say about marriage?

.... **(1 mark)**

Had a go ☐ Nearly there ☐ Nailed it! ☐

My future

Part-time jobs and money

Picture-based task: Working in a café

See this photo in colour

Keep your sentences short and use simple, accurate language. You don't need to write complicated phrases.

1 Describe the picture. Write four short sentences **in French**.

....

....

....

.... **(8 marks)**

A part-time job

2 Read this article that your Swiss friend, Lola, has written in her school magazine.

> Selon moi, avoir un petit emploi est très important pour les jeunes parce qu'on peut gagner de l'argent et ça nous permet de devenir plus indépendants. Moi, j'ai enfin trouvé un emploi dans un magasin de vêtements le week-end. Les heures sont longues et je ne m'entends pas bien avec ma patronne, mais c'est assez bien payé. La semaine dernière, j'ai acheté une jupe et un pantalon et j'étais vraiment contente. Le mois prochain, je vais dépenser mon argent avec des vacances à Paris!

What does Lola say?

Put a cross [×] next to each one of the **three** correct statements.

☐	A	Lola thinks that having a part-time job is a good idea.
☐	B	She works in an independent shop.
☐	C	Her hours are not long.
☐	D	She is quite well paid.
☐	E	Last week she bought some clothes.
☐	F	She went on holiday last month.

Read the question carefully and make sure you select the required number of answers. Here you need three.

(3 marks)

My future

Had a go ☐ Nearly there ☐ Nailed it! ☐

Opinions about jobs

Writing about jobs

1 Write to your friend about jobs.

You **must** include the following points:
- the importance of having a job
- your opinion of a job you want to do with reasons
- a recent part-time job
- where you would like to work in the future.

Write your answer **in French**. You should aim to write between 80 and 90 words.

> Remember to write accurately and cover the points with some complexity and variety.

....

....

....

....

....

....

....

(18 marks)

Views on work

2 Nadia and Yanis are talking about their views on work.

What do they say? Listen to the recording and complete the sentences by putting a cross [×] in the correct box for each question.

> When there are two parts to a question, the passages will be quite long, so you'll need to be attentive throughout.

Listen to the recording

Part 1

(a) Nadia says that her father ...
- ☐ **A** likes his job.
- ☐ **B** earns lots of money.
- ☐ **C** does not earn a lot of money.

(b) Nadia would like to work ...
- ☐ **A** in a café.
- ☐ **B** in a school.
- ☐ **C** as a professional sportswoman.

(c) Her current boss is ...
- ☐ **A** always smiling.
- ☐ **B** always strict.
- ☐ **C** always unpleasant.

Part 2

(a) Yanis would like to ...
- ☐ **A** live elsewhere.
- ☐ **B** be near his friends.
- ☐ **C** work in a village.

(b) Yanis was helped in his apprenticeship by ...
- ☐ **A** his pleasant boss.
- ☐ **B** the foreign tourists.
- ☐ **C** his ability to speak English.

(c) Because he likes going to sporting events, Yanis ...
- ☐ **A** doesn't want to work on Sundays.
- ☐ **B** wants to work at a stadium.
- ☐ **C** doesn't want to go to the tourist office.

(6 marks)

Had a go ☐   Nearly there ☐   Nailed it! ☐   **My future**

Job adverts and skills needed

Read aloud

1 Rachid, your friend from Canada, has sent you some information about jobs.

Read out the text below.

> Je travaille dans un magasin.
> J'aime tous les clients.
> On dit que je suis responsable et travailleur.
> Les heures ne sont pas trop longues.
> Je cherche un nouveau poste dans un très grand restaurant en ville.

(8 marks)

> Once you have read this aloud, listen to the recording in the Answer section to check your pronunciation and to practise any sounds or words you found difficult.

Follow-on questions

Once you have read the text aloud, listen to two questions related to what you have read.

You are expected to say a few words or a short phrase / sentence in response to each question. One-word answers will not be sufficient to gain full marks.   **(4 marks)**

> Keep your answers to the follow-on questions brief, but include a verb in each.

Job advertisement

2 You see this advertisement for a job.

> On cherche quelqu'un pour travailler à la caisse dans un petit supermarché à deux kilomètres de Rennes*. Nous voulons une personne qui est forte en maths et qui aime parler avec les clients. Envoyez un e-mail pour recevoir d'autres détails.

*Rennes is a town in France.

Answer the questions **in English**. You do not need to write full sentences.

(a) Where in the supermarket is the job?

....   **(1 mark)**

(b) Mention two qualities needed for the job.

....   **(2 marks)**

My future — Had a go ☐ Nearly there ☐ Nailed it! ☐

Applying for jobs

Role play

1 **Setting:** In a shop

   Scenario:
   - You are applying for a job in France.
   - Listen to the recording of the teacher's part.
   - The teacher will play the part of an employee and will speak first.
   - The teacher will ask questions **in French** and you must answer **in French**.
   - You are expected to say a few words or a short phrase / sentence in response to each prompt. One-word answers will not be sufficient to gain full marks.

   > **Task:**
   > 1 Say that you want a job.
   > 2 Ask about the salary.
   > 3 Say why you want to work in France.
   > 4 Say what you will do in the evenings after work.
   > 5 Ask a question about the hours.

   (10 marks)

   > Don't worry if you can't think of the translation of a particular word. Think of words you do know. For example, if you have forgotten the word for salary, how about *Combien payez vous*? Or *Je gagnerais combien*?

Picture-based task: Interviews

See this photo in colour

> Keep your sentences simple but accurate. There is no need to write complicated phrases for this question.

2 Describe the picture. Write four short sentences **in French**.

....
....
....
....

(8 marks)

Had a go ☐ Nearly there ☐ Nailed it! ☐   **My future**

Volunteering

Picture-based task: Volunteering

1 Describe the picture.

Your description must cover:
- people
- location
- activity.

See this photo in colour

(8 marks)

Follow-on questions

When you have finished your description, listen to the recording of two questions relating to your chosen picture. You are expected to say a few words or a short phrase / sentence in response to each question. One-word answers will not be sufficient to gain full marks.

(4 marks)

Volunteering

2 Lucas, Manon and Rachid are talking about volunteering.

What do they say?

Listen to the recording and complete the sentences by putting a cross [×] in the correct box for each question.

(a) Lucas has worked for a charity …

☐	A which helps cats.
☐	B for five months.
☐	C at a veterinary surgery.

(b) Manon …

☐	A volunteers to help the unemployed and homeless.
☐	B helps out with housework.
☐	C currently does not do voluntary work.

(c) Rachid …

☐	A works at café with computers.
☐	B used to do voluntary work.
☐	C helps out with school work.

(3 marks)

My future

Had a go ☐   Nearly there ☐   Nailed it! ☐

Equality and helping others

Helping others

1 Read Léa's blog about helping people.

> Je m'appelle Léa et je travaille avec les personnes âgées de mon quartier depuis deux ans. Elles ont besoin d'aide, mais elles méritent aussi d'être bien traitées. Je passe des heures à lire à une femme qui aura quatre-vingt-deux ans le mois prochain et elle me sourit chaque jour. Mon ambition est de créer plus d'égalité dans la société car je pense que c'est très important. Un jour, j'ai l'intention d'étudier le droit à l'université.

Complete the sentences below.

Put a cross [×] in the correct box for each question.

(a) Léa has been working with ...

☐ **A** old people.
☐ **B** unemployed people.
☐ **C** homeless people.

(b) She has spent hours ...

☐ **A** smiling.
☐ **B** reading.
☐ **C** feeling sad.

(c) Her ambition is to ...

☐ **A** create an equal society.
☐ **B** work with university students.
☐ **C** write a book.

(3 marks)

Translation

2 Translate the following five sentences **into French**.

(a) Equality is important.

....

(b) I like to help people.

....

(c) My parents give money to a local association.

....

(d) Last year I started to work with young people in town.

....

(e) I want to see a fair society where everybody is equal.

....

(10 marks)

> Remember to make your adjectives agree. 'Equality', 'charity' and 'society' are all feminine in French.

Had a go ☐ Nearly there ☐ Nailed it! ☐   **Environment**

The natural world

Picture-based task: The countryside

See this photo in colour

1 Describe the picture. Write four short sentences **in French**.

   ....

   ....

   ....

   ....

                                                                                                      (8 marks)

> Think about the people, what they are doing and where they are. If they are outside, as here, you could also write about the weather.

> Keep your answers simple for this task.

A visit to Africa

2 Léa has written an email about a recent visit.

> ✉
>
> J'ai passé une semaine à la campagne en Afrique avec mes copains. Dans le pays qu'on a visité, il ne pleut presque jamais et tout est très sec car il y fait toujours chaud, même en hiver. Malheureusement, il n'y a pas assez d'eau. Mes amis et moi sommes allés à un petit lac où les gens viennent afin de laver les vêtements.

What does Léa say?

Put a cross [×] next to each one of the **three** correct statements.

☐	A	Léa spent a month in Africa.
☐	B	The country she visited has lots of rainfall.
☐	C	The country is hot in winter.
☐	D	There is a lack of food.
☐	E	Léa went to a lake with her friends.
☐	F	People wash clothes in a lake.

> Make sure you read the whole passage carefully at least once before answering. The incorrect statements may contain some words taken from the passage.

(3 marks)

Environment   Had a go ☐   Nearly there ☐   Nailed it! ☐

Spending time in the countryside

Read aloud

1. Clara has contributed to a blog about the natural world.

   Read out the text below.

   > Je trouve la nature très intéressante.
   > Mes copains pensent qu'on doit sauver les arbres et les animaux.
   > Pendant les grandes vacances, je travaille dans une ferme.
   > Nous aimons passer du temps à la campagne à regarder les fleurs et de temps en temps, on fait de la natation dans un lac.

   (8 marks)

   > Remember that *aille* in *travaille* makes a sound like the y in the English word 'dry'. The letter combination *gn* in *campagne* is pronounced like the first part of the 'ni' sound in 'onion'.

   Follow-on questions

   Once you have read the text aloud, listen to two questions related to what you have read.

   You are expected to say a few words or a short phrase / sentence in response to each question. One-word answers will not be sufficient to gain full marks.

   (4 marks)

   > You can keep the answers to these questions short, but do answer in a sentence.

The natural world

2. Ahmed, Myriam and Clément are talking about the natural world.

   What do they say?

   Listen to the recording and complete the sentences by putting a cross [×] in the correct box for each question.

   (a) In the countryside, Ahmed likes …

☐	**A** swimming.
☐	**B** horse riding.
☐	**C** cycling.

   (b) Myriam likes looking at fish and …

☐	**A** rabbits.
☐	**B** horses.
☐	**C** chickens.

   (c) Clément says that there are fewer …

☐	**A** tourists.
☐	**B** buildings.
☐	**C** forests.

   (3 marks)

Had a go ☐ Nearly there ☐ Nailed it! ☐   **Environment**

The environment and me

Views on the environment

1 Lucas, Manon and Rachid are talking about the environment.

What do they say?

Listen to the recording and complete the following tables **in English**.

You do not need to write in full sentences.

(a) Lucas

His current thoughts about the environment

(b) Manon

Her recent action

(c) Rachid

His parents' opinions

(3 marks)

Translation

2 Translate the paragraph **into French**.

> I want to help the environment because I think that it's very important. I always recycle paper and glass. Last week my friends reused some plastic bags at the supermarket. We ought to reduce traffic in the towns and I am going to stop travelling by car in the future. We must not ignore pollution.

....
....
....
....
....
....
....
....
....

(10 marks)

Environment

Had a go ☐ Nearly there ☐ Nailed it! ☐

Local environmental issues

Helping the environment

1 Mathis is talking about helping the environment in a podcast.

What does he say?

Complete the gap in each sentence using a word or phrase from the box below.

There are more words / phrases than gaps.

bike	train	bus
by car	by bike	when it rains
an electric car	a bike	a house
proper	clean	popular

(a) Mathis prefers going into town by ………………………… .

(b) He never goes to school ………………………………… .

(c) In the future he is going to buy ………………………… .

Watch out for negatives.

(d) His friends think the town is ………………………………… .

(4 marks)

Local environmental issues

2 Théo has written a blog about local environmental issues.

What does Théo say about his local issues?

Put a cross [×] next to each one of the **three** correct statements.

> Je m'intéresse à l'environnement depuis quelques années et, il y a six mois, j'ai manifesté contre les déchets dans la ville. On trouve souvent des poissons morts dans le lac local car ils mangent le plastique jeté dans l'eau.

☐	A	Théo has been interested in the environment for some years.
☐	B	Théo cleaned up the local streets.
☐	C	Théo protested six months ago.
☐	D	Théo demonstrated about transport issues.
☐	E	Dead fish have been found in a lake.
☐	F	Fishing has been banned because of plastic waste.

(3 marks)

> Here, *depuis* and *il y a* are both used alongside periods of time, but you need to look at the tenses of the verbs used in the phrases, to see if those actions are ongoing or in the past:
>
> … *depuis* + present tense = to have been doing something for a time period, for example: *je suis professeur depuis 10 ans* = I have been a teacher for 10 years.
>
> … *il y a* + past tense = to have done something some time ago, for example: *il y a 3 ans je suis allé(e) à Paris* = 3 years ago I went to Paris.

Had a go ☐ Nearly there ☐ Nailed it! ☐   Environment

Global environmental issues

Dictation

1 You are going to hear someone talking about global environmental issues.

Sentences 1–2: write down the missing words in the gaps provided. In each gap, you will write one word **in French**.

1 Il y a des .... comme des ....

2 On doit recycler le ...., le .... et le ....

Sentences 3–6: write down the full sentences that you hear in the spaces provided, **in French**.

3 ....

4 ....

5 ....

6 .... **(10 marks)**

> In dictations, when you hear the three words from outside the vocabulary list, try to visualise how they would be written by listening to the sounds you hear.

Global environmental issues

2 Read this magazine article from a Belgian school magazine.

> Salut, tout le monde! Au collège, nous étudions les problèmes globaux et un scientifique* célèbre nous a raconté des catastrophes de l'environnement qui ont eu lieu dans des pays différents. Au Canada, il y a eu des inondations causées par le changement climatique et plus de cinquante mille animaux sont morts. C'était vraiment triste! Il a aussi parlé des espèces en danger en Afrique. Elles vont bientôt disparaître car elles ne vont pas trouver assez à manger et à boire.
>
> Nous pensons qu'on devrait protéger ces pauvres animaux. Il faut encourager les gens à ne pas jeter les déchets dans les rues, dans les parcs ou dans la mer parce que les animaux mangeront les choses en plastique et ils deviendront malades.

scientifique – scientist

Answer the following questions **in English**. You do not need to write in full sentences.

(a) What did the scientist talk about?

.... **(1 mark)**

(b) What has taken place in Canada and what were the consequences?

.... **(2 marks)**

(c) What problem did he talk about in Africa?

.... **(1 mark)**

(d) What does the writer say we should encourage people not to do?

.... **(1 mark)**

(e) What will happen to animals according to the last sentence? (Give **two** details.)

.... **(2 marks)**

Environment | Had a go ☐ Nearly there ☐ Nailed it! ☐

Caring for the planet

Talking about caring for the planet

1 As part of a conversation topic, you might be asked questions about the environment. Prepare answers to these questions and then speak for about 30 seconds on each one.

(a) Comment peut-on sauver notre planète?

(b) Qu'est-ce que tu as fait pour aider notre planète?

(c) Qu'est-ce que tu vas faire à l'avenir pour sauver notre planète?

> Don't worry if you can't think of any actual experience you've had for the conversation questions. Just use the French you know in your answer.

> Learn some flexible phrases that can be applied to many questions to help develop your conversation answers. Phrases such as *À mon avis …*, *On dirait que …*, *Par contre …*, *Cela vaut la peine …* are very useful when expressing opinion.

Translation

2 Translate the following sentences **into English**.

(a) J'aime beaucoup ma famille et mes amis.

....

(b) La planète est très importante pour moi.

....

(c) Nous devons aider les associations pour sauver la Terre.

....

(d) Hier, j'ai recyclé des choses en plastique.

....

(e) À l'avenir, je vais protéger les animaux en danger.

.... **(10 marks)**

> Make sure that you read each sentence fully before starting the translation. Consider each word, but remember that you may not always be able to translate word for word. Always read through to make sure that what you have written makes sense in English.

Had a go ☐ Nearly there ☐ Nailed it! ☐ **Environment**

A greener future

A letter about being green

1 Write to your friend about being green.

You **must** include the following points:
- transport in your area
- your opinion of public transport with reasons
- something you did recently to support the environment
- what you will do in the future to be greener.

Write your answer **in French**. You should aim to write between 80 and 90 words.

....
....
....
....
....
....
....
....
....
....

(18 marks)

A greener future

2 Jade has written an email about a greener future.

> ✉
>
> Nous devons tous agir afin de protéger notre monde, sinon on risque de voir disparaître beaucoup d'espèces d'animaux et de ne pas avoir assez d'espaces verts. Ce serait terrible! À mon avis, il ne faut pas permettre aux gens de construire trop de bâtiments à la campagne, surtout si cela détruit le beau paysage. Nous sommes en train de perdre trop de beaux champs! Je crois qu'il est important de soutenir la nature et de convaincre les gens que la situation actuelle est grave et que nous devons devenir plus conscients de l'effet de nos actions sur l'environnement!

Answer the following questions **in English**. You do not need to write in full sentences.

(a) What two consequences are mentioned if people don't act together to save the world?

.... **(2 marks)**

(b) What shouldn't people be allowed to do in the countryside?

.... **(1 mark)**

(c) How does she describe the current situation?

.... **(1 mark)**

About the exams

Had a go ☐   Nearly there ☐   Nailed it! ☐

Practice for Paper 1: Speaking

Practise for the Speaking tasks with this selection of exam-style questions.

Role play

1 **Setting: In a hotel**

   Scenario: You are at a hotel in France.
   - Listen to the recording of the teacher's part.
   - The teacher will play the part of an employee at the hotel and will speak first.
   - The teacher will ask questions **in French** and you must answer **in French**.
   - You are expected to say a few words or a short phrase / sentence in response to each prompt. One-word answers will not be sufficient to gain full marks.

   > **Task:**
   > 1 Say how long you would like to stay.
   > 2 Say how many people are staying.
   > 3 Say what meals you want.
   > 4 Say why you are in France.
   > 5 Ask a question about facilities.

   (10 marks)

Read aloud

2 Manon, your friend from Belgium, has sent you some information about herself.

   Read out the text below.

   > Je suis très sportive.
   > Je vais au collège en car.
   > Je fais du vélo avec ma famille.
   > Le dimanche, je joue au foot avec mes amis.
   > J'aime boire du café et manger des pâtes.

   Once you have read the text aloud, listen to two questions related to what you have read.

   You are expected to say a few words or a short phrase / sentence in response to each question. One-word answers will not be sufficient to gain full marks.

   (4 marks)

Picture-based task: In the classroom

3 Describe the picture.

   Your description must cover:
   - people
   - location
   - activity.

   See this photo in colour

   When you have finished your description, listen to the recording of two questions relating to your chosen picture. Pause the recording to give your answer.

   Then continue the recording to hear questions from the conversation section of the task on the broader thematic context of **Studying and my future**.

   (12 marks)

Had a go ☐ Nearly there ☐ Nailed it! ☐   **About the exams**

Practice for Paper 1: Speaking

Practise for the Speaking tasks with this selection of exam-style questions.

Role play

1 **Setting: In town**

   Scenario:
   - You are in a town in France with your family and you speak to a passer-by.
   - Listen to the recording of the teacher's part.
   - The teacher will play the part of the passer-by and will speak first.
   - The teacher will ask questions **in French** and you must answer **in French**.
   - You are expected to say a few words or a short phrase / sentence in response to each prompt. One-word answers will not be sufficient to gain full marks.

   Task:
   1 Say where you want to visit.
   2 Say what you think of the town centre.
   3 Ask for directions to a place you want to visit.
   4 Say what you want to do there.
   5 Ask about transport options.

   (10 marks)

Read aloud

2 Luis has contributed to a blog about healthy living. Read out the text.

   > Je veux manger plus de légumes.
   > J'essaie de faire beaucoup de sport, surtout en été.
   > J'évite de passer trop de temps devant un écran car je pense que c'est vraiment malsain.
   > Demain, mes copains vont faire du vélo à la campagne, mais moi, je vais faire de la natation avec mes deux sœurs.

   (8 marks)

   Once you have read the text aloud, listen to two questions related to what you have read. You are expected to say a few words or a short phrase / sentence in response to each question. One-word answers will not be sufficient to gain full marks. **(4 marks)**

Picture-based task: A family meal

3 Describe the picture.

   Your description must cover:
   - people
   - location
   - activity.

   When you have finished your description, listen to two questions relating to your picture. You are expected to say a few words or a short phrase / sentence in response to each question. One-word answers will not be sufficient to gain full marks. **(4 marks)**

   Then continue the recording to hear questions from the conversation section of the task on the broader thematic context of **My personal world**. You will be asked questions in the present, past and future tenses. Your responses should be as full and detailed as possible.

   (8 marks)

Practice for Paper 2: Listening

Had a go ☐ **Nearly there** ☐ **Nailed it!** ☐

Practise for the Listening tasks with this selection of exam-style questions.

A description of a town

1. Manon is talking about her town.

   Which things does she mention? Listen to the recording and put a cross [×] in each one of the **three** correct boxes.

☐ **A** a castle	☐ **D** transport
☐ **B** clean streets	☐ **E** a stadium
☐ **C** shops	☐ **F** a swimming pool

   (3 marks)

Rachid's family

2. Rachid is talking about his family. What does he say? Listen to the recording and complete the sentences by putting a cross [×] in the correct box for each question.

   (a) Rachid does not get on well with …

☐ **A** his brother.
☐ **B** his sister.
☐ **C** his uncle.

   (b) His sister …

☐ **A** is too chatty.
☐ **B** is not nice.
☐ **C** is older than him.

   (c) His uncle …

☐ **A** lives in France.
☐ **B** is very sporty.
☐ **C** is English.

   (d) His uncle doesn't like …

☐ **A** travelling.
☐ **B** sport.
☐ **C** reading.

   (e) His aunt finds her job …

☐ **A** dull.
☐ **B** interesting.
☐ **C** exciting.

   (5 marks)

Talking about holidays

3. Nathan is talking about holidays.

   What does he say? Listen to the recording and answer the following questions **in English**. You do not need to write in full sentences.

   (a) Where does Nathan's family prefer to go on holiday? ....

   (b) Where is their next holiday going to be? ....

   (2 marks)

4. Jade and Pierre are talking about holiday accommodation options. What do they like and dislike? Listen to the recording and complete the following tables **in English**. You do not need to write in full sentences.

   (a) Jade …

likes:	
dislikes:	

   (b) Pierre …

likes:	
dislikes:	

   (4 marks)

Had a go ☐   Nearly there ☐   Nailed it! ☐

About the exams

Practice for Paper 2: Listening

Practise for the Listening tasks with this selection of exam-style questions.

Target grade 4-5

Track 77

A holiday destination

1 Listen to this advert promoting the holiday destination of Villeneuve. What is mentioned?

   Listen to the recording and put a cross [×] in each one of the **three** correct boxes.

☐	A transport	☐	D eating out
☐	B accommodation	☐	E weather
☐	C shopping	☐	F sports

   (3 marks)

Target grade 6-8

Track 78

A discussion between friends

2 Théo and Myriam are talking about their lives. What do they say? Listen to the recordings and complete the sentences by putting a cross [×] in the correct box for each question.

   (a) Théo needs …

☐	A extra money.
☐	B to sell items.
☐	C to make new friends.

   (b) He has …

☐	A several jobs.
☐	B so much school work.
☐	C an office job.

   (c) Théo will be available to work …

☐	A in the summer.
☐	B every day.
☐	C after school.

   (d) Currently Myriam …

☐	A is taking exams.
☐	B is finding school hard.
☐	C has no homework.

   (e) She has been working in a shop …

☐	A for six months.
☐	B for a month.
☐	C with a vet.

   (f) Her parents …

☐	A are not responsible.
☐	B are worried about their jobs.
☐	C think that Myriam is not ambitious.

   (6 marks)

Target grade 4-9

Track 79

Dictation

3 You are going to hear someone talking about healthy living.

   Sentences 1–2: write down the missing words in the gaps provided. In each gap, you will write one word **in French**.

   1 Le .... est l' ....

   2 J'aime .... le .... et la ....

   Sentences 3–6: write down the full sentences that you hear in the spaces provided, **in French**.

   3 ....

   4 ....

   5 ....

   6 ....

   (10 marks)

About the exams

Had a go ☐ Nearly there ☐ Nailed it! ☐

Practice for Paper 3: Reading

Practise for the Reading tasks with this selection of exam-style questions.

Internet comments

1 Read these comments from an internet forum.

> **Alex:** J'aide mes parents à la maison. Je travaille dans le jardin et je fais la cuisine.
>
> **Clara:** Le week-end je sors avec mes amis. On va souvent au cinéma mais je n'aime pas aller à la piscine.
>
> **Enzo:** Je fais de la natation le week-end avec mes parents. Le dimanche nous regardons un match de foot à la télé.

Who says what? Choose the correct answers.

Put a cross [×] in the correct column for each question.

	Who …	Alex	Clara	Enzo
(a)	… watches sport?			
(b)	… prepares food?			
(c)	… works in the garden?			
(d)	… watches films?			
(e)	… goes swimming?			
(f)	… goes out with friends?			

(6 marks)

An email from a friend

2 Read this email from Luis to his friend.

> ✉
> Salut!
> Je pense que les vacances sont importantes. On peut se reposer, et mes parents disent que c'est amusant de passer du temps ensemble à l'étranger.
> L'année dernière, nous sommes allés en Angleterre et c'était génial, mais il a beaucoup plu. J'ai visité un musée d'art et un vieux château historique. C'était intéressant! Malheureusement, nous n'avons pas fait les magasins!
> Demain, je vais en ville avec mes amis pour visiter le stade.
> Tu aimes aller en vacances?
> Luis

Complete the gap in each sentence using a word from the box below.

There are more words than gaps.

> great   rainy   cloudy
> the shops   the stadium   a castle   his friend's house

(a) The weather in England was ....

(b) Luis visited ....

(c) Tomorrow he is going to visit ....

(3 marks)

90

Had a go ☐ Nearly there ☐ Nailed it! ☐

About the exams

Practice for Paper 3: Reading

Practise for the Reading tasks with this selection of exam-style questions.

Future plans

1 Read Marie's plans for the future.

> Je m'appelle Marie. Je vais bientôt avoir seize ans et j'ai commencé à penser de mon avenir. Puisque je suis forte en langues au collège, j'ai toujours voulu travailler à l'étranger, mais je sais qu'il est difficile de trouver un bon emploi. Je suis travailleuse et je fais toujours de mon mieux, alors j'espère réussir dans la vie. J'ai trouvé un poste dans un supermarché près de chez moi et je gagne un peu d'argent, mais à l'avenir, je voudrais devenir *infirmière* car j'adore aider les malades et j'aimerais travailler dans un hôpital.

Complete the sentences below. Put a cross [×] in the correct box for each question.

(a) Marie will soon be …

☐	**A** 15.
☐	**B** 16.
☐	**C** 14.

(b) She has always wanted to …

☐	**A** be good at languages.
☐	**B** work in a school.
☐	**C** work abroad.

(c) She describes herself as …

☐	**A** hard working.
☐	**B** serious.
☐	**C** the best pupil in her school.

(d) She has found …

☐	**A** supermarket shopping hard.
☐	**B** a part-time job.
☐	**C** some money.

(e) Which of these is the best translation for the word *infirmière*?

☐	**A** nurse
☐	**B** accountant
☐	**C** banker

(5 marks)

A blog

2 Read Louis's blog.

> Je viens de passer deux jours dans une grande ville du sud de la France avec ma classe de français. Après avoir trouvé des renseignements sur l'histoire de la ville à la bibliothèque le matin, nous avons visité une vieille tour et un pont avant de passer le premier après-midi sur la côte où nous avons étudié le sable et les causes du changement climatique. Le lendemain, j'ai fait des recherches dans un musée en ville, mais après, nous avons pu nous reposer un peu. On a visité un parc où on a vu des animaux en liberté et on a chanté et dansé sur la plage le soir. Je me suis très bien amusé, et je voudrais bien retourner à cette ville un jour.

Complete the sentences below. Put a cross [×] in the correct box for each question.

(a) On the first day Louis went first to …

☐	**A** an old tower.
☐	**B** a bridge.
☐	**C** the library.

(b) On the first afternoon, he …

☐	**A** studied sand.
☐	**B** danced on the beach.
☐	**C** noticed a change in the weather.

Answer these questions **in English**. You do not need to write in full sentences.

(c) What did Luis do first on the second day? ………………………………………

(d) What was special about the animals in the park he visited? ………………………………………

(4 marks)

About the exams

Had a go ☐   Nearly there ☐   Nailed it! ☐

Practice for Paper 4: Writing

Practise for the Writing tasks with this selection of exam-style questions.

Target grade 1-5

Picture-based task: A group of friends

1 Describe the photo. Write four short sentences **in French**.

  ....
  ....
  ....
  ....

(8 marks)

See this photo in colour

Target grade 1-5

A review

2 Write a review of a shopping centre for a website.

  You **must** include the following points:
  - where the shopping centre is
  - your opinion of the shops
  - when you will next visit the shopping centre.

  Write your answer **in French**. You should aim to write between 40 and 50 words.

  ....
  ....

Continue your answer on your own paper.

(14 marks)

Target grade 1-5

Writing about your family and friends

3 Write to your friend about your family and friends. You **must** include the following points:
  - what your family is like
  - your opinion of your best friend with reasons
  - what you did with your friends last week
  - where you will go next week with your family.

  Write your answer **in French**. You should aim to write between 80 and 90 words.

Write your answers to this question on your own paper.

(18 marks)

Target grade 1-5

Translation

4 Translate the following five sentences **into French**.

  (a) I love my town.

  ....

  (b) My house is very big.

  ....

  (c) I play football in the garden.

  ....

  (d) Last week I went to the shops with my brother.

  ....

  (e) I can go cycling on Saturday in the countryside.

  ....

(10 marks)

Had a go ☐ Nearly there ☐ Nailed it! ☐

About the exams

Practice for Paper 4: Writing

Practise for the Writing tasks with this selection of exam-style questions.

Target grade 4-9

Writing about your holidays

1 Write to your friend about your holidays.

You **must** include the following points:
- why holidays are important
- your opinion of holidays abroad with reasons
- how you spent your last holidays
- where you will go this summer.

Continue your answer on your own paper.

Write your answer **in French**. You should aim to write between 80 and 90 words.

....
....
....
....
....

(18 marks)

Writing about technology

2 Write about technology for an online magazine.

You **must** include the following points:
- what technology you use
- the pros and cons of the internet
- what you did last week online
- how you will use technology this weekend.

You can finish writing your answers to longer writing questions on your own paper.

Write your answer **in French**. You should aim to write between 130 and 150 words.

....
....
....
....
....
....
....

(22 marks)

Translation

3 Translate the paragraph **into French**.

> I like going to school. My favourite subject is English. I always do my homework in my bedroom before eating. Last week my friends and I went to the museum in town. I am going to study at university in the future because I want to find a very good job.

....
....
....

(10 marks)

Grammar

Had a go ☐ Nearly there ☐ Nailed it! ☐

Articles 1

To say 'the' in French you use *le*, *la*, *l'* or *les* in front of the noun. Remember that in French every noun has a gender. Objects are either masculine (m) or feminine (f) and are singular or plural.

A Put in the correct word for 'the' (*le*, *la*, *l'*, *les*) in front of these nouns. They are all places around a town.

Example: la banque (f)

1 .... magasins (pl)
2 .... pharmacie (f)
3 .... toilettes (pl)
4 .... hôtel (m)
5 .... cinémas (pl)
6 .... musée (m)
7 .... gare (f)
8 .... parking (m)
9 .... rues (pl)
10 .... appartement (m)

To say 'a' or 'an' in French, you use *un* or *une* depending on whether the noun is masculine or feminine.

B Show that you understand when to put *un* or *une* in front of the following words.

1 .... frère (m)
2 .... famille (f)
3 .... sœur (f)
4 .... père (m)
5 .... tante (f)
6 .... mère (f)
7 .... oncle (m)
8 .... fils (m)

C Fill in the gaps in this table, paying attention to the articles: *un*, *une*, *des*, *le*, *la*, *l'*, *les*.

Singular	Plural
	les chiens
un château	
l'animal	
	des voitures
le nez	
le bateau	
un hôtel	
l'arbre	les arbres
	des pages
	les eaux
une piscine	
	les villes

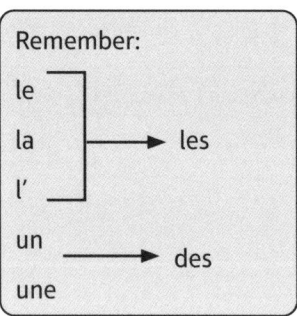

Remember:
le ⎫
la ⎬ → les
l' ⎭
un ⎫
une ⎭ → des

Had a go ☐ **Nearly there** ☐ **Nailed it!** ☐   Grammar

Articles 2

> If you want to say 'some' or 'any' in French, you use the partitive article *du*, *de la*, *des* or *de l'*, depending on the gender of the noun you are talking about.

A Put the correct word for 'some' in front of these nouns. Pay attention to the genders in brackets.

1 ……… fromage (m)
2 ……… eau (f)
3 ……… frites (pl)
4 ……… café (m)
5 ……… légumes (pl)
6 ……… pain (m)
7 ……… œufs (pl)
8 ……… viande (f)
9 ……… poisson (m)
10 ……… pâtes (pl)

B Unfortunately, you have nothing left to eat or drink in the house. Using the example below, answer the following questions, then translate them **into English**.

e.g. Tu as du pain? *Je n'ai pas de pain. I haven't any bread.*

> Always use *de …* (or *d' …*) on its own after a negative in French to say 'any'. There is no need to put *du*, *de la*, *de l'* or *des*.

1 Tu as des œufs? ………………………………………………………………………
2 Tu as du thé? …………………………………………………………………………
3 Tu as de l'eau? ………………………………………………………………………
4 Tu as de la viande? …………………………………………………………………
5 Tu as du sucre? ………………………………………………………………………

C Fill in the gaps to show where you are going. Use *au*, *à l'*, *à la* or *aux*.

1 Je vais ……… gare. (f)
2 Je vais ……… café. (m)
3 Je vais ……… magasins. (pl)
4 Je vais ……… piscine. (f)
5 Je vais ……… banque. (f)
6 Je vais ……… collège. (m)
7 Je vais ……… hôpital. (m)
8 Je vais ……… parcs. (pl)
9 Je vais ……… école. (f)
10 Je vais ……… marché. (m)

Grammar

Had a go ☐   Nearly there ☐   Nailed it! ☐

Adjectives

Adjectives are used to describe nouns. Remember that in French you need to ensure they have the correct endings depending on whether the noun is masculine, feminine, singular or plural.

A Circle the correct form of the adjectives.

1 Ma mère est petit / petite.

2 Mon père est grand / grande.

3 Ma maison est beau / belle.

4 Mon chat est noir / noire.

5 Elle est heureux / heureuse.

6 Les fenêtres sont chère / chères.

B Using the adjectives in the box, complete the sentences below. Don't forget to change them to the feminine or plural form where necessary.

1 Mon chien est ……………………………………………………………… (large)

2 Mes stylos sont ……………………………………………………………… (white)

3 Ma mère est ……………………………………………………………… (hard-working)

4 Mes frères sont ……………………………………………………………… (sporty)

5 Mes sœurs sont ……………………………………………………………… (sad)

6 Ma tante est très ……………………………………………………………… (pleasant)

> gros
> blanc
> travailleur
> sportif
> triste
> agréable

C Complete this table with all the different forms of the adjectives.

masc. sing.	fem. sing.	masc. plural	fem. plural	English
grand	grande		grandes	big / tall
	petite			
noir		noirs		
	neuve		neuves	
		derniers		last
marron		marron		
triste		tristes		sad
sérieux		sérieux		
	active	actifs		
amusant		amusants		funny
	vieille		vieilles	old
	belle	beaux		
ancien		anciens		ancient
blanc		blancs		white
	sportive		sportives	

D Make sentences that use the adjectives in **C** above. Make sure they have the correct form and are in the correct position.

Example: J'ai deux chemises (grand, gris) *J'ai deux grandes chemises grises.*

1 Elle a des yeux (beau, bleu). …………………………………………………

2 Les fleurs (meilleur, jaune). …………………………………………………

3 Mes baskets (vieux, blanc). …………………………………………………

4 Mes parents (pauvre, malade). …………………………………………………

> Most adjectives come **after** the noun but some come **before**, e.g. *grand*.

Had a go ☐ **Nearly there** ☐ **Nailed it!** ☐

Grammar

Possessives

A Do the four activities below on possessives.

> To say something is 'my', 'his', etc, you use a possessive adjective e.g. *mon, ma, mes*.

1 Choose *mon*, *ma* or *mes* to fill in the gaps.

Dans ma famille, il y a mon père, ... mère, ... sœur et .... deux frères. .... grand-mère vient souvent chez nous avec .... grand-père. .... amie adore .... grands-parents.

2 Use *son*, *sa* or *ses* to fill in the gaps.

Dans sa chambre, elle a .... lit, ... livres, ... bureau, ... télévision, ... vêtements, ... portable et .... sac.

3 Use *notre / notre / nos* to translate 'our' or *votre / votre / vos* to translate 'your'.

Dans notre collège, nous avons .... professeurs, ... bibliothèque, ... cour et .... terrain de sport. Et vous, qu'est-ce que vous avez dans .... collège et dans .... salles de classe? Vous avez .... tableaux blancs et .... gymnase?

4 Your teacher asks you questions about yourself. Insert the correct word for 'your'.

(a) Comment s'appellent .... père et .... mère?

(b) Qu'est-ce que tu achètes avec .... argent?

(c) C'est quand .... anniversaire?

(d) Qu'est-ce qu'il y a dans .... ville ou .... village?

5 How would you talk about what they have in **their** town?

Dans leur ville, ils ont .... hôtel, ... cinémas, ... pharmacie, ... boulangerie, ... cafés, ... parcs, ... hôpital, ... école et tous .... petits magasins.

B How many grammatically correct but silly sentences can you make from this table?

mon / ma / mes	fromage	est	très	jaune(s)
ton / ta / tes	amies	n'est pas	assez	triste(s)
son / sa / ses	vélo	sont		moderne(s)
notre / nos	gâteaux	ne sont pas		grand(e)(s)
votre / vos	football			agréable(s)
leur / leurs	photos			juste(s)

....
....
....
....
....
....
....

Grammar

Had a go ☐ Nearly there ☐ Nailed it! ☐

Comparisons

> Use the comparative form of the adjective to say 'more than' or 'less than':
>
> *plus* + adjective + *que* or *moins* + adjective + *que*
>
> Use the superlative form of the adjective to say 'the most' or 'the least':
>
> *le / la / les* + *plus / moins* + adjective
>
> In both cases, the adjective ending must agree with the noun it refers to.

A Work out who is the biggest and the smallest: Marie, Lucie or Tom.

Marie est grande.

Marie est plus grande que Tom.

Tom est moins grand que Lucie.

Lucie est plus grande que Marie.

Tom n'est pas aussi grand que Marie.

Qui est le / la plus grand(e)? ....

Qui est le / la moins grand(e)? ....

B Using the grades below, make up four sentences about how these students compare in each subject.

Example: En anglais, Anna est meilleure qu'Antoine.

	Antoine	Anna	
Anglais	3	6	....
Français	7	4	....
Histoire	4	2	....
Technologie	6	9	....

C Put each of these sentences in the correct order, then translate them.

Example: est que courte plus jupe Ma jupe ta   Ma jupe est plus courte que ta jupe.

My skirt is shorter than your skirt.

1 aussi est Sara grand Philippe que ....

2 maths que plus musique Les difficiles sont la ....

3 Les moins sont les saines fruits frites que ....

4 Une est moins un confortable cravate qu' pantalon ....

5 l' science que est intéressante aussi anglais La ....

Had a go ☐ Nearly there ☐ Nailed it! ☐   Grammar

Other adjectives and pronouns

A Put the correct word in each gap: *ce*, *cette*, *cet* or *ces*.

1 .... jupe
2 .... pantalon
3 .... robe
4 .... chaussures
5 .... chapeau
6 .... veste
7 .... chaussettes
8 .... hôtel
9 .... maison
10 .... hôpital

ce = this (m)
cet = this (in front of a masculine noun beginning with a vowel)
cette = this (f)
ces = these (pl)

B Select the correct form of the interrogative adjective 'which' (*quel*, *quelle*, *quels* or *quelles*) for each question.

1 .... est ta matière préférée?

2 .... montagne est la plus haute du monde?

3 .... temps fait-il aujourd'hui?

4 Ils ont écouté .... chanteur ce soir?

5 .... viandes mangez-vous?

6 .... garçons est-ce que tu vois?

7 .... livre préfères-tu?

8 Ta sœur doit faire .... devoirs?

C Select the correct form of either the indefinite adjective *autre* (other) or *quelque* (some) to complete the sentence.

autre (m)	quelque (m)
autre (f)	quelque (f)
autres (mpl)	quelques (mpl)
autres (fpl)	quelques (fpl)

Indefinite adjectives also need to agree with the noun they describe.

1 Il lisait le livre pendant .... temps.

2 Je voudrais recevoir .... cadeaux chers pour mon anniversaire.

3 Mon .... voiture est noire et très vieille.

4 Son .... sœur va au lycée avec son voisin.

5 Attention! Il est facile de parler en ligne avec .... personne inconnue.

6 J'ai acheté d' .... vêtements dans le magasin.

7 Sa mère a mangé .... frites avant de sortir.

8 Je n'aime que les maths et le français, mais mon ami préfère les .... matières.

Grammar

Had a go ☐ Nearly there ☐ Nailed it! ☐

Adverbs

> Adverbs are used to describe the verb. In French a lot of adverbs end in **-ment**.

A Form adverbs from these adjectives.

1 malheureux ……………..
2 extrême …………………
3 probable …………………
4 vrai ……………………..
5 certain ………………….
6 complet ………………..

B Underline all the adverbs in this paragraph, then translate it. Use the English translations in the box if you are stuck.

first	in the future
often	usually
then	next
finally	so

Le matin, <u>d'abord</u>, je me lève à sept heures, puis d'habitude, je prends mon petit-déjeuner. Ensuite, je quitte la maison. Finalement, j'arrive au collège à huit heures et demie, mais c'est souvent trop tôt. Alors, à l'avenir, je vais rester au lit plus longtemps.

In the morning, ………………………………………………………………………………………
………………………………………………………………………………………………………
………………………………………………………………………………………………………

C Fill in the gaps from this passage with the best adverb from the box. There may be more than one answer. The first letter of the adverb has been given for you.

Généralement je vais en France avec mes parents et mon petit frère pour les grandes vacances. S…………….. mes grands-parents viennent avec nous, et c'est v…………….. pratique car ils font r…………….. du baby-sitting. Cependant, de …………….., ils se sentent v…………….. fatigués et ils ne sont pas t…………….. à l'aise, d…………….. ils ne viendront pas l'année prochaine. À l'avenir, ils viendront s…………….. s'ils sont a…………….. en forme!

absolument
de temps en temps
~~généralement~~
donc
régulièrement
sans doute
seulement
souvent
toujours
vraiment

D Write four sentences of your own with at least one adverb in each.

………………………………………………………………………………………………………
………………………………………………………………………………………………………
………………………………………………………………………………………………………
………………………………………………………………………………………………………

Had a go ☐ Nearly there ☐ Nailed it! ☐   **Grammar**

Object pronouns

Direct object pronouns are words like 'it', 'me', 'him', 'us', etc. You use them when you don't want to keep repeating a noun or a name.

A Translate these sentences.

Example: Il me regarde. *He watches me.*

1 Nous te voyons. ....
2 Tu le connais? ....
3 Je veux la voir. ....
4 Vous nous rencontrez. ....
5 Elle vous oubliera. ....
6 Je les perdrai. ....

You use **indirect** object pronouns to replace a noun which has *à* (*au*, *aux*, etc) in front of it.

B Translate the following sentences. Notice that in English we sometimes omit the 'to'.

Example: Il me donne un billet. *He gives me a ticket. / He gives a ticket to me.*

1 Je te passe mes livres. ....
2 Ne lui parle pas. ....
3 Nous lui offrirons un portable. ....
4 Il va nous envoyer un cadeau. ....
5 Tu leur raconteras l'histoire. ....

Translate *lui* as 'him' and 'her', and *leur* as 'them'.

C Put the words in the correct order to answer the question.

Example: Tu aimes les animaux?   je beaucoup aime les Oui   *Oui, je les aime beaucoup.*

1 Vous comprenez le professeur?   le souvent comprenons Nous
....

2 Elle aime les sports d'hiver?   pas aime Elle ne du tout les
....

3 Tu vas vendre ton vélo?   vendre vais le Oui je demain
....

4 Il veut acheter la maison?   veut pas il acheter ne Non l'
....

In the perfect tense, the pronoun comes before the auxiliary verb (*avoir* or *être*). The past participle needs to agree with the object pronoun, so if the object is feminine or plural, the past participle must end in *-e*, *-s* or *-es*. *Je les ai acheté(e)s* I bought them.

D Replace the underlined noun with a pronoun and move it to the correct position in the sentence.

Example: J'ai mangé le gâteau. *Je l'ai mangé.*

1 Il cherche les clés. ....
2 Nous envoyons un cadeau à Jeanne. ....
3 Il a donné des livres aux enfants. ....
4 Tu as téléphoné à tes amis? ....

Grammar

Had a go ☐ Nearly there ☐ Nailed it! ☐

More pronouns: *y* and *en*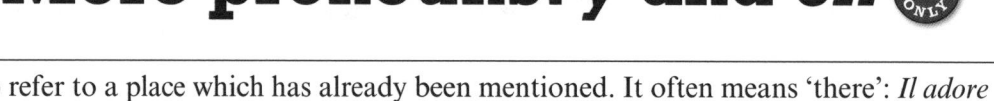

You use *y* to refer to a place which has already been mentioned. It often means 'there': *Il adore Paris. Il y est allé hier.* You also use it with verbs that take *à*. It can also be used instead of an indirect pronoun as in sentence 3.

A Replace the nouns with the pronoun y.

Example: Tu vas **au cinéma** ce soir? Tu y vas ce soir?

1 Il va habiter **au Canada**. ....

2 Elle a vu ses amis **en France**. ....

3 Vous jouez **au tennis**? ....

4 Je suis arrivé **au collège** avant les autres. ....

5 Tu es allée **au travail** ce matin? ....

You use *en* to replace a noun. It often means 'of it', 'of them' or 'some':
J'aime le chocolat. J'en mange beaucoup.

B Unjumble these sentences with *en* in order to answer the questions.

Example: Tu as de l'argent?   ai j' Oui en   Oui j'en ai

1 Tu fais beaucoup de sport?   en beaucoup J' fais

   ....

2 Elle fait du vélo?   pas en fait n' Elle

   ....

3 Vous avez deux frères?   trois ai Non en j'

   ....

4 Ils mangent de la viande tous les jours?   les en samedis Ils tous mangent

   ....

5 Il y a des bouteilles dans la cuisine?   y en Il a plusieurs

   ....

C Replace the nouns in brackets with either *y* or *en*.

> Using pronouns makes your work more interesting and for your GCSE, if you are aiming for higher grades, you should try to use them.

1 Je vais (au restaurant) de temps en temps.

....

2 J'adore les fruits et je mange beaucoup (de fruits).

....

3 J'aime le chocolat mais je ne mange jamais (de chocolat) parce que c'est mauvais pour la santé.

....

4 Je suis allé (au théâtre) la semaine dernière avec mon frère.

....

5 On va au concert ce soir. Tu veux aller (au concert)?

....

6 Moi, j'adore la viande, mais mon frère ne mange pas (de viande) parce qu'il est végétarien.

....

Had a go ☐ **Nearly there** ☐ **Nailed it!** ☐

Grammar

Other pronouns

Relative pronouns are used when you want to link statements together to avoid repetition and to make your French more fluent.

A Fill in the gaps with *qui* (followed by a verb), or *que / qu'* (followed by a subject / person).

Example: C'est le bruit *que* je n'aime pas.

1 Le repas ……………. j'ai pris était excellent.

2 C'est Claude ……………. est le plus beau.

3 Ce sont mes parents ……………. adorent la viande.

4 Voilà le chapeau ……………. il a perdu.

5 Où sont les robes ……………. sont bleues?

6 La tour ……………. j'ai visitée était vieille.

7 L'homme ……………. monte dans le train est petit.

8 Ma copine ……………. s'appelle Mathilde a seize ans.

9 Quel est le film ……………. tu veux voir?

> *Qui* means 'which', 'who' or 'that' and replaces the subject in a sentence.
> *Que* means 'whom', 'which' or 'that' and replaces the object in the sentence.

> *Dont* replaces 'whose' or 'of whom / which', for example:
> *Je veux voir le film **dont** j'ai vu la bande-annonce.*
> I want to see the film whose trailer I saw.

B Which would you use: *y*, *en*, *où*, *qui* or *que*? Insert the correct pronoun and translate the sentences into English.

1 Le repas ……………. nous avons mangé était excellent.

………………………………………………………………………………………………………

2 Les pâtes? J'……………. ai mangé beaucoup.

………………………………………………………………………………………………………

3 Le café ……………. je vais le samedi est fermé.

………………………………………………………………………………………………………

4 Le cinéma Gaumont? J'……………. suis allée pour voir 'Les Minions'.

………………………………………………………………………………………………………

Grammar

Had a go ☐   Nearly there ☐   Nailed it! ☐

Present tense: -er verbs

A Give the *je*, *nous* and *ils* forms of each of these verbs.

Verb	je (j')	nous	ils
aimer	j'aime	nous aimons	ils aiment
donner			
habiter			
inviter			
jouer			
marcher			
parler			
quitter			
regarder			
trouver			

B Use the verbs above to write how you would say:

Example: he likes il aime

1 you (pl) speak ....
2 she invites ....
3 you (s) live ....
4 we find ....
5 he looks at ....

6 you (pl) walk ....
7 you (s) give ....
8 she leaves ....
9 he plays ....
10 they look at ....

> Although the verbs below are -*er* verbs, they are slightly irregular in that the spelling often changes. For example, *manger* becomes *mangeons* in the *nous* form.

C Put the verbs in brackets in the correct form and watch out for the spelling.

-ger verbs

1 ils (bouger) ....
2 nous (télécharger) ....
3 nous (changer) ....
4 je (manger) ....

-ler / -ter verbs

1 je (s'appeler) ....
2 ils (jeter) ....
3 nous (se rappeler) ....
4 elle (s'appeler) ....

-yer verbs

5 tu (envoyer) ....
6 vous (payer) ....
7 j' (essayer) ....
8 nous (envoyer) ....

acheter-type verbs

5 tu (acheter) ....
6 elles (préférer) ....
7 vous (se lever) ....
8 il (acheter) ....

D Fill in the correct part of the verb in these questions and translate them.

Example: Tu (parler) français? Tu parles français? Do you speak French?

1 Ils (habiter) en France? ....
2 Marie (manger) de la viande? ....
3 Vous (préférer) la science? ....
4 Les sœurs (jeter) les fruits? ....
5 Mon copain et moi (acheter) des frites? ....

Had a go ☐   Nearly there ☐   Nailed it! ☐   **Grammar**

Present tense: -*ir* and -*re* verbs

-*ir* and -*re* verbs are another set of verbs which follow a regular pattern. It is important to learn the most common verbs.

A What do these -*ir* verbs mean? Match the French to the English.

finir	to warn
prévenir	to succeed
remplir	to think about
agir	to obtain
réussir	to finish
obtenir	to act
choisir	to fill
réfléchir	to choose

Remember, both -*ir* and -*re* verbs can be either regular or irregular. Be careful to learn how each group behaves (*Revision Guide* page 105). On this page, the **irregular** verbs have stars. Keep them separate in your vocabulary lists to help you remember which is which.

B Fill in the gaps in this table. (The verbs are irregular.)

	dormir*	**sortir***
je		sors
tu	dors	
il / elle		sort
nous		
vous		sortez
ils / elles	dorment	

C Put the correct ending on these -*ir* verbs to make them match their subjects.

Example: Ils (réussir) à trouver un cadeau. *Ils réussissent à trouver un cadeau.*

1 L'ami (choisir) un cadeau. ....
2 Vous (courir*) aux magasins. ....
3 Nous (finir) nos devoirs. ....
4 Je (remplir) le verre d'eau. ....

Be careful, many of the regular -*ir* verbs, such as *choisir* and *finir*, add -is, -is, -it, -issons, -issez, -issent.

D Complete the table below.

	vendre	**prendre***	**écrire***
je			
tu	vends		
il / elle			
nous		prenons	écrivons
vous		prenez	
ils / elles	vendent		

E Give the correct present tense form of the verb in brackets.

1 nous (vendre) ....
2 ils (répondre) ....
3 je (descendre) ....
4 tu (prendre*) ....
5 vous (boire*) ....
6 elle (lire*) ....
7 je (traduire*) ....
8 il (comprendre*) ....

Grammar

Had a go ☐   Nearly there ☐   Nailed it! ☐

Avoir and *être*

A Give the correct part of *avoir* in these sentences.

Example: Tu as un frère?

1 Elle .... un chat.
2 J'............... les cheveux blonds.
3 Ils .... une grande maison.
4 Il .... onze ans.
5 Nous .... un petit appartement.
6 Vous .... un beau chien.
7 Ma sœur .... une jupe rouge.
8 Les filles .... un problème.
9 Tu .... deux livres.
10 Vous .... une nouvelle maison.

B Translate the following sentences **into French**.

Example: We have a house in Paris.   Nous avons une maison à Paris.

1 They have a dog and three cats.   ....
2 Do you (s) have a sister?   ....
3 She has black hair.   ....
4 We have a big kitchen.   ....
5 I have three children.   ....
6 I am sixteen years old.   ....
7 He has a car.   ....

C Fill in the gaps with the correct part of *être*.

Example: Il est très amusant.

1 Je .... français.
2 Nous .... tristes.
3 Ma tante .... assez petite.
4 Vous .... sportif mais calme.
5 Mes yeux .... bleus.
6 Tu .... content?
7 Les chiens .... grands.
8 Je .... au chômage.
9 Nous .... canadiens.
10 Il .... agréable.

D Write six sentences using *être* or *avoir* and words from the grid below.

Je	maison	noirs	petit
Tu	yeux	bleu	professeur
L'homme	grand	amusant	court
Nos chiens	canadiens	cheveux	chapeau
Vos parents	rouge	voiture	marron
Les filles	triste	long	gros

....
....
....
....
....
....

> Remember, when you are using the verb *être* you need to make sure the adjective agrees with the noun!

Had a go ☐ **Nearly there** ☐ **Nailed it!** ☐   Grammar

Reflexive verbs

A Add the correct reflexive pronoun.

1 Je .... lève.

2 Tu .... reposes.

3 Il .... amuse.

4 Elles .... appellent.

> se reposer – to rest
> Je me repose
> Tu te reposes
> Il / elle / on se repose
> Nous nous reposons
> Vous vous reposez
> Ils / elles se reposent

B Write the correct perfect tense of each verb.

Example: Je (s'amuser) = Je me suis amusé(e).

1 Je (se couper) la main.

2 Elle (se marier).

3 Nous (se lever) à huit heures.

4 Il (se demander) pourquoi.

5 Tu (s'amuser) beaucoup.

C Match up the French and English.

1 On s'amuse	A They rest
2 Ils se reposent	B It takes place
3 Je m'entends	C We get up
4 Il se passe	D I get on
5 Je m'intéresse	E Your name is
6 Nous nous levons	F We enjoy ourselves
7 Tu t'appelles	G I wonder
8 Je me demande	H I'm interested

Grammar

Had a go ☐ Nearly there ☐ Nailed it! ☐

Other important verbs

> The verbs *devoir* (to have to / must), *pouvoir* (to be able to / can), *vouloir* (to want to) and *savoir* (to know) are known as **modal verbs**.

A Complete this table with the correct part of the modal verb.

	devoir	pouvoir	vouloir	savoir
je	dois			sais
tu		peux		
il / elle / on			veut	
nous	devons			savons
vous			voulez	
ils / elles		peuvent		

B Rearrange the words to make correct sentences.

Example: la dois prendre Je première rue Je dois prendre la première rue.

1 mon -vous Pouvez père aider? ....
2 nager -tu Sais? ....
3 maison acheter parents une veulent Mes nouvelle ....
....
4 s'arrêter feu On toujours doit au rouge ....
5 moi avec ce Voulez danser soir -vous? ....
6 sait écrire lire Elle et déjà ....

C Change the verb to match the new subject given in italics.

Example: Il doit travailler dur et moi aussi, *je* dois travailler dur.

1 Elle veut trouver une chambre et nous aussi, *nous* ....
2 Les élèves peuvent louer un vélo et toi aussi, *tu* ....
3 Le pilote doit tout vérifier et vous aussi, *vous* ....
4 Elle sait faire la cuisine, et eux aussi, *ils* ....
5 Je peux faire du vélo et elles aussi, *elles* ....
6 Il ne peut jamais comprendre les règles et vous non plus, *vous* ....
7 Nous savons préparer les repas et moi aussi, *je* ....

D Make up six sentences about school from this table.

	(ne) doit (pas)	manger en classe.
		porter ses propres vêtements.
	(ne) peut (pas)	courir dans l'école.
On		répondre aux professeurs.
	(ne) veut (pas)	dormir en classe.
		jeter les livres en classe.
	(ne) sait (pas)	parler aux autres élèves.
		envoyer des textes.

Had a go ☐ Nearly there ☐ Nailed it! ☐   **Grammar**

The perfect tense 1

You use the perfect tense to talk about single events in the past. It is formed by using the present tense of *avoir* + past participle.

A Create your own sentences using a word or words from each column.

J'ai	fini	le gâteau
Tu as	détesté	le bateau
Il a	vendu	les devoirs
Elle a	regardé	l'argent
Nous avons	mangé	la maison
Vous avez	attendu	le bus
Ils ont	choisi	les chiens
Elles ont	perdu	le pain

B Add the correct part of *avoir* to complete these sentences.

Example: Samedi soir, j'ai regardé la télé.

1 Elle .... invité sa copine au match.
2 Vous .... fini le repas?
3 Ils .... travaillé au collège.
4 Il .... beaucoup neigé ce matin.
5 Tu n'............... pas mangé de légumes?
6 Nous .... choisi un bon restaurant.
7 Elle n'............... pas oublié son livre.
8 Ils .... attendu à l'aéroport.
9 J'............... visité le musée.
10 Nous n'............... pas entendu le bruit.

C Did you notice the position of the *ne ... pas* in exercise B to say that they did **not** do something? Using the table in exercise A to help you, how would you say the following?

Example: You (s) did not sell the house. Tu n'as pas vendu la maison.

1 We did not lose the money. ....
2 You (pl) did not wait for the dogs. ....
3 I did not finish the bread. ....
4 She did not sell the boat. ....
5 He did not hate the homework. ....

D Revise the irregular past participles, then fill in the gaps in these sentences.

Example: Il a vu la voiture. (voir)

1 J'ai .... le livre sur la table. (mettre)
2 Elle a .... à son frère. (écrire)
3 Tu n'as rien .... au collège? (faire)
4 Il n'a pas .... ma lettre. (lire)
5 Nous avons .... acheter une voiture. (pouvoir)

E Complete these sentences with the correct part of *avoir* and the past participle of the verb given.

1 J'............... la situation. (comprendre)
2 Il .... un chien. (voir)
3 Tu .... un bus à la gare ? (prendre)
4 Qu'est-ce que tu ....? (faire)

Grammar

Had a go ☐   Nearly there ☐   Nailed it! ☐

The perfect tense 2

> The perfect tense can also be formed using the verb *être* + past participle, when the verb is reflexive and with 14 verbs of movement.

A Add the correct part of the verb *être* to complete these sentences.

Example: Tu *es* né en 2000?

1 Elle .... tombée.
2 Mes copains .... arrivés trop tard.
3 Les chats .... montés sur la table.
4 Marie n'............... pas descendue vite.
5 Emma .... allée à la piscine.
6 Vous .... retournés en France?
7 Je ne .... pas parti tôt.
8 Elles .... entrées dans la maison.

B Make the past participle match the subject of these *être* verbs, by adding agreements (-, -*e*, -*s*, -*es*) to those that need it.

Example: Mes cousines sont rest*ées* à l'hôtel.

1 Élise est arrivé .... à 11 heures.
2 Il est allé .... au collège.
3 Nous sommes entré ...., tous les garçons, dans le magasin.
4 Marie n'est rentré .... qu'à minuit.
5 Mes stylos ne sont pas tombé ....
6 Il est sorti .... avec sa sœur.

C Complete the sentences.

Example: Je suis allé au collège et elle aussi, elle *est allée au collège.*

1 Tu es monté très vite et les filles aussi, elles ....
2 Les hommes sont arrivés et moi aussi, je ....
3 Nous ne sommes pas tombés et eux non plus, ils ....
4 Il est allé en ville et sa soeur aussi, elle ....

(H only — applies to questions 3)

D Complete this table to show a reflexive verb in the perfect tense.

je	me	suis	levé
tu		es	
il			
elle			levée
nous		sommes	
vous			
ils	se		levés
elles			

Reflexive pronouns:
me   nous
te   vous
se   se

E Form the perfect tense of these reflexive verbs.

Example: Je (se demander) pourquoi. = Je me suis demandé(e) pourquoi.

1 Elle (se reposer) sur la plage. ....
2 Ils (se lever) à 7 heures. ....
3 Je (s'entendre) bien avec mon frère. ....
4 Elles (s'intéresser) à l'histoire. ....

Had a go ☐   Nearly there ☐   Nailed it! ☐   **Grammar**

The imperfect tense

The imperfect is another tense that you use to talk about the past. You use it to describe what happened over a period of time, what something was like and ongoing actions which were interrupted.

A Give the imperfect (*je*, *nous* and *ils* forms) of these verbs.

1 jouer	je jouais	nous jouions	ils jouaient
2 finir	je finissais	nous finissions	ils finissaient
3 perdre	....	....	....
4 avoir	....	....	....
5 être	....	....	....
6 boire	....	....	....
7 aller	....	....	....
8 partir	....	....	....
9 faire	....	....	....
10 lire	....	....	....
11 savoir	....	....	....
12 prendre	....	....	....

B Change the ending of the imperfect tense to match the new subject.

Example: Il jouait et nous aussi, nous jouions.

1 J'attendais et elle aussi, elle ....
2 Vous écriviez et eux aussi, ils ....
3 Tu dormais et le chien aussi, il ....
4 Mes parents regardaient et moi aussi, je ....
5 Mon ami était content et mes sœurs aussi, elles ....

> All verbs except *être* are regular in the imperfect tense.
> **1** Take the *nous* form of the present tense and take off the *-ons* ending: *nous habit(ons)*.
> **2** Add the imperfect endings:
> j'habitais   nous habitions
> tu habitais   vous habitiez
> il / elle   ils / elles
> habitait   habitaient

C Put the verbs into the imperfect tense, then translate the sentences.

Example: Tu visitais beaucoup de monuments. (visiter)
You used to visit lots of monuments.

1 Je .... avec mon petit frère sur la plage. (jouer) ....
2 Nous .... très souvent ensemble. (manger) ....
3 Il .... dans l'école. (travailler) ....
4 On .... beaucoup de glaces. (vendre) ....
5 Ils .... du vélo. (faire) ....
6 Tu .... très content. (être) ....

D When you are talking or writing about the past, you often need to use a mixture of perfect tense and imperfect tense verbs. Put the following verbs in the correct past tense.

J'[aller] au collège quand j'[voir] mon ami. Il y [avoir] beaucoup de gens. J'[dire] « Bonjour ».

Grammar

Had a go ☐ Nearly there ☐ Nailed it! ☐

The future tense

> The **near future** is used to say what is going to happen. It is formed using *aller* + infinitive.

A Complete the sentences with the correct part of *aller*, then write the translation.

Example: Je vais regarder un film. I am going to watch a film.

1 Il .... sortir ce soir. ....
2 Nous .... vendre la maison. ....
3 Vous .... bientôt comprendre. ....
4 Tu .... partir en vacances. ....
5 Ma mère .... voir un concert. ....
6 Les garçons .... arriver en retard. ....

B Unjumble these sentences in the near future tense.

Example: ta Je à question vais répondre Je vais répondre à ta question.

1 aller allons en Nous ville demain ....
2 partir Quand vas-tu? ....
3 vont leurs Ils devoirs faire ....
4 tennis allez au jouer Vous? ....
5 Théo cuisine faire la va ....
6 aider Ses vont sœurs ....

> The **future** is used to say what you **will** do. To form it, add these endings to the infinitive: *-ai, -as, -a, -ons, -ez, -ont*.

C Say what everyone will do at the weekend. Put the verb into the future tense.

Example: Je *mangerai* le petit-déjeuner. (manger)

1 Il .... sa nouvelle voiture. (laver)
2 Tu .... ton amie à manger. (inviter)
3 Je .... mes devoirs. (finir)
4 Vous .... le bus. (manquer)
5 Elle .... sa tante. (visiter)
6 Ils .... en France. (arriver)
7 Elles .... beaucoup. (parler)
8 Je .... au foot demain. (jouer)

D Now try these irregular verbs. Check you know the irregular stem.

Example: vous (pouvoir) vous pourrez

1 ils (devoir) ....
2 nous (savoir) ....
3 je (faire) ....
4 elle (être) ....
5 tu (avoir) ....
6 elles (venir) ....
7 il (voir) ....
8 tu (aller) ....

E Now translate all of exercise D into English.

Example: You will be able to

1 ....
2 ....
3 ....
4 ....
5 ....
6 ....
7 ....
8 ....

Had a go ☐ Nearly there ☐ Nailed it! ☐   **Grammar**

The conditional tense

The conditional is used to say what you **would** do. It is formed like the future but has different endings. The conditional endings are: -ais, -ais, -ait, -ions, -iez, -aient.

For Foundation level, you only need to know *Je voudrais*; *Tu voudrais* and; *Il / Elle / On voudrait*.

You also need these forms at Higher level, plus *je*, *tu* and *il / elle / on* forms of *aller*, *avoir*, *être* and *faire*, and all forms of -*er* verbs.

A Complete the gaps in this table. For Higher tier only

	vouloir
je	
tu	
il / elle	

aller	avoir	être	faire	-er verbs (e.g. jouer)
irais				
		serais		jouerais
	aurait		ferait	

Remember for Higher tier you will also need to know the *nous*, *vous* and *ils / elles* forms of -*er* verbs.

B What would these people do if they won the lottery? Add the correct part of the verb in brackets and say what the sentence means **in English**.

Example: J'irais en vacances avec ma famille. (aller)

I would go on holiday with my family.

1 Ma mère .... une belle maison. (habiter) ....

2 Vous ne .... plus. (travailler) ....

3 Nous .... beaucoup de pays. (visiter) ....

4 Il .... de l'argent aux autres. (donner) ....

5 .... -tu mettre de l'argent à la banque? (vouloir) ....

6 J' .... une nouvelle voiture. (acheter) ....

C Complete these sentences using the conditional of the verb in brackets. They all have irregular stems, but they keep the same endings as above.

Example: Il ferait une sortie. (faire)

1 Je .... très riche. (être)

2 Est-ce que tu .... de la natation? (faire)

3 Il .... beaucoup d'amis. (avoir)

4 Elle .... en France. (aller)

D Write four *si* sentences of your own, using either the future or conditional tense.

Be careful with 'if' clauses!

si + present tense + future tense:
*Si tu y **vas**, moi aussi j'**irai**.*
If you go, I will go too.

....

....

....

si + imperfect tense + conditional:
*Si tu **mangeais** bien, tu n'**aurais** pas faim.*
If you ate well, you wouldn't be hungry.

....

....

....

Negatives

A Match the French to the English translations.

French	English
ne … pas	neither … nor
ne … jamais	not any, none
ne … rien	not yet
ne … personne	no longer, no more
ne … aucun	never
ne … que	nothing, not anything
ne … ni … ni …	not
ne … pas encore	only
ne … plus	nobody, not anybody

(ne … jamais → never)

B Translate these sentences.

Example: Il ne parle pas de sa famille.   He doesn't talk about his family.

1 Nous n'aimons ni la science ni l'histoire. ....
2 Je ne mangerai plus de viande. ....
3 Il n'est jamais arrivé. ....
4 Ils n'ont rien trouvé. ....
5 Je n'envoie aucun e-mail. ....
6 Elle ne fait que deux heures par mois. ....
7 Il ne retournera plus jamais en France. ....

C Rearrange the words to make correct sentences.

Example: n' personne vu Je ai   Je n'ai vu personne

1 ai aucun n' Je problème ....
2 ne jamais au Il va musée ....
3 Elles pas contentes ne sont ....
4 n' rien Il bu a ....
5 vais ne acheter pas Je de viande ....

D Make these sentences negative by inserting the given words. Remember that *du, de la, de l', des, un* and *une* all change to *de (d')* and mean 'any' if they appear after the negative.

Example: Je vois un chien dans la rue (ne … pas)   Je ne vois pas de chien dans la rue

1 Nous mangerons des légumes (ne … plus) ....
2 Elle a dit bonjour (ne … jamais) ....
3 Tu rencontres deux amies en ville (ne … que) ....
4 Il a compris (ne … rien) ....

Had a go ☐   Nearly there ☐   Nailed it! ☐

Grammar

The perfect infinitive and the present participle

A Give the perfect infinitive of the following verbs.

Example: manger *avoir mangé*

1 faire ....
4 mettre ....

2 jouer ....
5 vouloir ....

3 finir ....
6 écrire ....

B Match up the French and the English.

1 Après avoir joué au foot, …	A After having eaten, …
2 Après avoir mangé, …	B After having done my homework, …
3 Après avoir pris le train, …	C After having drunk a coffee, …
4 Après avoir fait mes devoirs, …	D After having read a book, …
5 Après avoir lu un livre, …	E After having taken the train, …
6 Après avoir bu un café, …	F After having played football, …

C Translate these sentences **into French**.

After having chosen the vegetables, she prepared a meal. ....

After having eaten, he went to the cinema. ....

After chatting to his friends, he went home. ....

After having lost her keys, she cried. ....

D Translate these sentences **into French**.

1 Before doing her homework, she downloaded some music. ....

2 Before returning, he bought a map. ....

3 Before leaving, he danced. ....

4 Before going out, he phoned his mother. ....

E Put these infinitives into the present participle.

1 finir ....
6 faire ....

2 acheter ....
7 prendre ....

3 aller ....
8 avoir ....

4 dire ....
9 partir ....

5 manger ....
10 venir ....

F Complete the sentences by changing the verb in brackets into the present participle.

1 J'ai lu un livre en (écouter) de la musique. ....

2 Elle lui a expliqué la situation en (rire). ....

3 Nous avons réussi en (travailler) beaucoup. ....

4 Ils sont entrés dans la maison en (courir). ....

5 Ma mère a bu de l'eau en (regarder) la télé. ....

Grammar

Had a go ☐   Nearly there ☐   Nailed it! ☐

The passive (H)

A Match up the correct English and French.

1 La lettre a été écrite par mon grand-père.	A The meals are made by my father.
2 Les repas sont faits par mon père.	B The money was given by my aunt.
3 Les animaux ne sont pas acceptés.	C The film was watched by everyone.
4 L'argent a été donné par ma tante.	D The emails will be sent tomorrow.
5 Le film a été regardé par tout le monde.	E The letter was written by my grandfather.
6 Les e-mails seront envoyés demain.	F Pets are not accepted.

B Translate the following **into English**.

1 Les hommes étaient invités à la fête. ....

2 Je suis toujours aidé par mes professeurs. ....

3 Mon appartement a été vendu. ....

4 Les livres ont été achetés. ....

5 L'histoire était écrite. ....

C Translate the following **into French**.

1 The house will be sold. ....

2 The door has been opened. ....

3 The fruit has been eaten. ....

4 The dogs are loved. ....

5 The drinks are ordered. ....

Had a go ☐ **Nearly there** ☐ **Nailed it!** ☐   Grammar

Questions

In French you can make something a question by raising your voice at the end of a sentence. However, if you are aiming for a Higher grade you need to use question words.

A Make these sentences into questions by using *est-ce que*.

Example: Tu manges des frites.   Est-ce que tu manges des frites?

1 Il peut venir lundi. ....

2 Vous avez une carte de la ville. ....

3 Les élèves ont fini leurs devoirs. ....

4 Elle veut aller en ville. ....

5 Vous êtes professeur. ....

6 Nous allons arriver au collège à huit heures. ....

B Find the five pairs of questions which mean the same.

1 Est-ce que tu aimes le français?   A Fait-il du français le mardi?

2 Est-ce qu'elle est française?   B As-tu français le mardi?

3 Est-ce qu'il adore le français?   C Aimes-tu le français?

4 Est-ce que tu as français le mardi?   D Est-elle française?

5 Est-ce qu'il fait du français le mardi? E Adore-t-il le français?

C Match the question word with the rest of the sentence.

1 Qu'   A es-tu venu?

2 Combien de   B est-ce que tu aimes faire?

3 Où   C est-ce que tu vas aider les pauvres?

4 Comment   D habites-tu?

5 Pourquoi   E préférez-vous voyager en France? En train?

6 À quelle heure   F parles-tu français?

7 Depuis quand   G est-ce que tu te lèves le matin?

8 Quand   H personnes habitent à Paris?

D Imagine you get the chance to interview your favourite celebrity. Prepare a list of six questions for them.

....

....

....

....

....

....

Speaking (Foundation)

Had a go ☐   Nearly there ☐   Nailed it! ☐

Pearson Edexcel publishes official Sample Assessment Material on its website. This test has been written to help you practise what you have learned across the four skills and may not be representative of a real exam paper.

Read aloud

My personal world

1 Sarah, your friend from Belgium, has sent you some information about herself. Read out the text below.

> J'ai quinze ans.
> Je suis assez petite.
> On dit que je suis travailleuse.
> J'aime beaucoup faire du sport avec mes amis.
> Le samedi je vais en ville en bus ou je vais au cinéma.

Track 80

Now listen to the recording of two questions related to what you have read. You are expected to say a few words or a short phrase / sentence in response to each question. One-word answers will not be sufficient to gain full marks.   **(12 marks)**

Role play

2 **Setting:** At the shop
   Scenario: You are in a gift shop in France.

Track 81

Listen to the recording of the teacher's part. The teacher will play the part of the shop assistant and will speak first. They will ask questions **in French** and you must answer **in French**. You are expected to say a few words or a short phrase / sentence in response to each prompt. One-word answers will not be sufficient to gain full marks.

> **Task:**
> 1 Say what you want.
> 2 Say who the item is for.
> 3 Say what the occasion is.
> 4 Give your opinion of the item you have been shown.
> 5 Ask about the price.

(10 marks)

Picture-based task

Picture 1

See this photo in colour

Picture 2

See this photo in colour

Track 82

3 Describe **ONE** of these pictures. Your description must cover:

   • people   • location   • activity.

Now listen to the recording. You will hear two questions related to each picture above. Answer the two questions related to your chosen picture. You are expected to say a few words or a short phrase / sentence in response to each question. One-word answers will not be sufficient to gain full marks.   **(12 marks)**

Track 83

You will then move on to a conversation on the broader thematic context of **Studying and my future**. Play the recording of an example of a teacher's question. In the real exam, your teacher will ask you more than one question. Practise saying your answer – it should be as full and detailed as possible and could use a variety of tenses.   **(16 marks)**

TOTAL FOR PAPER = 50 MARKS

Had a go ☐ Nearly there ☐ Nailed it! ☐

Practice papers

Listening (Foundation)

Holidays

1 Ahmed, Myriam and Clément are talking about holidays. What do they say? Listen to the recording and complete the sentences by putting a cross [×] in the correct box for each question.

(a) Ahmed goes on holiday with …

☐	A his friends.
☐	B his cousins.
☐	C his family.

(b) Myriam likes to …

☐	A go swimming.
☐	B go cycling.
☐	C go to the beach.

(c) Clément often goes to …

☐	A Canada.
☐	B England.
☐	C France.

(3 marks)

School subjects

2 Emma is talking about her school subjects. Which items does she mention? Listen to the recording and put a cross [×] in each one of the **three** correct boxes.

| ☐ | A History | ☐ | C Music | ☐ | E Science |
| ☐ | B Maths | ☐ | D English | ☐ | F French |

(3 marks)

Relationships

3 Lucas is talking about his family. What does he say? Complete the gap in each sentence using a word or phrase from the box below.

There are more words / phrases than gaps.

> on Saturdays   on Sundays   in the park
> hard-working   strict   chatty
> chores   homework   downloading

(a) Lucas and his brother play football………………… .

(b) His stepsister is too…………………………… .

(c) Lucas's mother helps him with………………… .

(3 marks)

Food and drink

4 Eva is talking about food and drink. What does she mention?

Listen to the recording and put a cross [×] in each one of the **three** correct boxes.

| ☐ | A pasta | ☐ | C meat | ☐ | E vegetables |
| ☐ | B fish | ☐ | D coffee | ☐ | F milk |

(3 marks)

Tourist attractions

5 Rachid is talking about his region. What does he say? Listen to the recording and complete the sentences by putting a cross [×] in the correct box for each question.

(a) Rachid lives …

☐	A at the seaside.
☐	B in the mountains.
☐	C in a village.

(b) There are lots of tourists …

☐	A all year round.
☐	B in summer.
☐	C in spring.

(c) In town people visit …

	A	the castle.
	B	the shops.
	C	the museum.

(d) There is a tower …

	A	in the town centre.
	B	10 kilometres away.
	C	2 kilometres away.

(4 marks)

A hotel

Track 89

6 Inès is at a hotel, asking for information. What does the employee say? Listen to the recording and complete the following tables **in English**. You do not need to write in full sentences.

(a)	The number of rooms in the hotel	
(b)	The restaurant's speciality	
(c)	The restaurant's daily closing time	

(3 marks)

Healthy lifestyles

Track 90

7 Clara is talking about healthy lifestyles. What does she say? Listen to the recording and complete the sentences by putting a cross [×] in the correct box for each question.

(a) Clara does sport …

	A	once a week.
	B	twice a week.
	C	twice a day.

(b) Her brother prefers …

	A	doing exercise.
	B	video games.
	C	going cycling.

(c) Last week Clara …

	A	went swimming.
	B	ate healthy food.
	C	played on her computer.

(3 marks)

The environment

Track 91

8 Hugo is talking about helping the environment in a podcast. What does he say? Complete the gap in each sentence using a word or phrase from the box below.

There are more words / phrases than gaps.

> on foot   by bus   by car
> loves   never uses   hates
> by train   by bike   by car
> nothing   everything   paper
> plastic   paper   nothing

(a) When Hugo goes to town, he travels ……………… .

(b) His mother …………………… her electric car.

(c) When it rains, Hugo travels ………………… to school.

(d) Hugo's brother recycles ………………………………… .

(e) His parents recycle …………………………………… .

(5 marks)

A new shopping centre

Track 92

9 Listen to this advert promoting a shopping centre. What is mentioned? Listen to the recording and put a cross [×] in each one of the **three** correct boxes.

	A	car parks		D	places to eat
	B	transport		E	children's play area
	C	having a rest		F	supermarkets

(3 marks)

Had a go ☐ Nearly there ☐ Nailed it! ☐

Practice papers

Free-time activities

Track 93

10 Clément, Yasmina and Mohamed are talking about their free-time activities. What do they say? Listen to the recording and complete the sentences by putting a cross [×] in the correct box for each question.

(a) Clément likes going to …

☐	A town.
☐	B the beach.
☐	C visit his mother.

(b) Yasmina goes to the swimming pool …

☐	A after school.
☐	B every day.
☐	C with her friends.

(c) From time to time Yasmina goes to the countryside to …

☐	A go cycling.
☐	B walk with friends.
☐	C visit a castle.

(d) On Friday Mohamed is going to …

☐	A go to a party.
☐	B celebrate a birthday.
☐	C buy a present.

(4 marks)

School life

Track 94

11 (a) Nathan is talking about school life. What does he say?

Listen to the recording and answer the following questions **in English**. You do not need to write in full sentences.

(i) What does Nathan think about his teachers? .... **(1 mark)**

(ii) What did he do yesterday evening? .... **(1 mark)**

(b) Jade and Pierre are talking their likes and dislikes at school. What do they like and dislike?

Listen to the recording and complete the following tables **in English**. You do not need to write in full sentences.

(i) Jade …

| likes … | |
| dislikes … | |

(ii) Pierre …

| likes … | |
| dislikes … | |

(4 marks)
(Total for Question 11 = 6 marks)

Dictation

Track 95

12 You are going to hear someone talking about themselves and their friends.

Sentences 1–3: write down the missing words in the gaps provided. In each gap, you will write one word **in French**.

Example: Moi j'ai seize ans.

1 Je .... assez ....

2 J'ai .... yeux ....

3 Mon .... est très ....

Sentences 4–6: write down the full sentences that you hear in the spaces provided, **in French**.

Example: J'aime le football.

4 ....

5 ....

6 ....

(10 marks)

TOTAL FOR PAPER = 50 MARKS

121

Practice papers

Had a go ☐   Nearly there ☐   Nailed it! ☐

Reading (Foundation)

Holidays

1   Read these comments from an internet forum.

> **Alex:** En été, je vais en vacances au Canada avec ma famille. On fait les magasins.
>
> **Enzo:** Moi, je visite le sud de la France avec mes amis. On fait du sport ensemble.
>
> **Clara:** Je vais en Angleterre en avion avec mon ami. On voit un match de foot.

Who says what? Choose the correct answers.

Put a cross [×] in the correct column for each question.

	Who …	Alex	Enzo	Clara
(a)	goes to England?			
(b)	does sport?			
(c)	goes shopping?			
(d)	goes on holiday with their family?			
(e)	visits the south of France?			
(f)	watches sport?			

(6 marks)

A restaurant

2   Read the advertisement.

> Nouveau restaurant au centre-ville, près du pont. Cinquante tables, service excellent.
> Ouvert de seize heures à onze heures du soir. Menus à 30, 50 et 75 euros.
> Pas de petit-déjeuner ou de déjeuner. Idéal pour les familles ou les touristes.
> Chiens acceptés.

Put a cross [×] in each one of the **three** correct boxes.

The restaurant …

☐	**A** is near the harbour.		☐	**D** doesn't serve breakfast.
☐	**B** is open from 3pm.		☐	**E** is ideal for tourists.
☐	**C** has three different priced menus.		☐	**F** does not accept dogs.

(3 marks)

A village

3   Read the extract from a local village brochure.

> Le beau village est populaire avec tout le monde. On peut visiter la vieille tour et un petit musée d'art. Il y a aussi un petit supermarché, une pharmacie et une *boucherie* où on achète de la viande locale.

Had a go ☐ **Nearly there** ☐ **Nailed it!** ☐

Practice papers

(a) Complete the sentences below.

Put a cross [×] in the correct box for each question.

(i) In the village you can visit …

☐	**A**	a tower.
☐	**B**	a castle.
☐	**C**	a swimming pool.

(ii) There is also …

☐	**A**	a bakery.
☐	**B**	a large supermarket.
☐	**C**	a chemist's.

(b) Which of these is the best translation for the word ***boucherie***?

Put a cross [×] in the correct box.

☐	**A**	bank
☐	**B**	butcher's shop
☐	**C**	station

(3 marks)

The environment

4 Read these comments from Emma and Yanis on an internet forum.

> **Emma:** Je déteste ma région. Je pense qu'il y a beaucoup de voitures et de bruit au centre-ville. Ma mère dit que les rues ne sont pas propres et que c'est dangereux.

> **Yanis:** Je recycle tous les jours car il est important d'aider l'environnement. Je respecte les associations dans ma région qui aident les autres, mais selon moi, le plus grand problème au monde, c'est la pollution.

(a) Emma

One thing she says about the town centre ………………………………………….. .

One opinion her mother gives ……………………………..…………………………… . **(2 marks)**

(b) Yanis

What Yanis does every day …………………………………………………………… .

The biggest world problem according to Yanis ……………………………………… .

(2 marks)

(Total for Question 4 = 4 marks)

A celebrity

5 Read the article from a French newspaper.

> Vous êtes tous invités au concert de musique gratuit par le chanteur français Magman*. Le concert se passe le 9 août à dix-neuf heures dans le parc du centre-ville.
>
> Le concert va durer deux heures. Vous pouvez acheter des vêtements et des cadeaux pour aider une association qui protège les animaux.
> À dix heures du soir on va organiser une fête!

Magman – fictional singer

Practice papers

Had a go ☐ Nearly there ☐ Nailed it! ☐

Put a cross [×] in each one of the **three** correct boxes.

☐	A	The concert is taking place in July.	☐	D	Pets are allowed at the concert.
☐	B	The concert is free.	☐	E	The concert is raising money for charity.
☐	C	The concert is will last for 2 hours.	☐	F	You are advised to bring warm clothes.

(3 marks)

School trips

6 Read the email that Hugo wrote to his French friend.

> Salut!
>
> J'aime mon collège car je m'entends bien avec les élèves et les professeurs et on fait beaucoup de voyages scolaires. Le mois dernier, je suis allé au stade dans une grande ville avec ma classe et on a participé à une journée de sport. Moi, j'ai joué au foot et mon équipe a gagné. C'était passionnant!
>
> L'année prochaine, nous allons en France pour regarder un match de basket à Paris.
>
> Tu fais des visites scolaires?
>
> Hugo

Complete the gap in each sentence using a word from the box below.

There are more words than gaps.

> headteacher   friends   students
> lost   won   drew
> next month   next year   in March

(a) Hugo gets on well with the teachers and ………………………… .

(b) At the sports day, his team ………………………………… .

(c) He is going to France ………………………………………… .

(3 marks)

Future plans

7 Read Mathis's blog about the future.

> Je m'appelle Mathis et j'ai commencé à penser de mon avenir. J'ai toujours voulu devenir professeur, mais la formation est très longue et quand je vois les jeunes de mon quartier qui ne respectent pas la planète, j'ai changé d'avis.
>
> J'ai l'intention de trouver un petit travail car j'ai besoin de l'argent pour acheter des vêtements, des jeux vidéo et peut-être un nouveau portable, mais plus tard, je voudrais trouver un métier intéressant. Maintenant je crois que je voudrais être **comptable**, comme ma mère qui travaille dans une banque, parce que j'aime les maths.

(a) Complete the sentences below.

Put a cross [×] in the correct box for each question.

(i) Mathis has started to think about …

☐	A	his school.
☐	B	his future.
☐	C	his friends.

(ii) He thinks that teachers …

☐	A	work long hours.
☐	B	have a long training period.
☐	C	like children.

Had a go ☐ **Nearly there** ☐ **Nailed it!** ☐   Practice papers

(iii) He intends to …

☐	**A** get a part-time job.
☐	**B** save the planet.
☐	**C** sell mobile phones.

(iv) He would like to …

☐	**A** find an interesting job.
☐	**B** find a well-paid job.
☐	**C** work with children.

(b) Which of these is the best translation for the word *comptable*?

Put a cross [×] in the correct box.

☐	**A** teacher
☐	**B** baker
☐	**C** accountant

(5 marks)

A diary entry

8 Marie writes in her diary.

> Ce matin à huit heures et demie, je suis allée en ville avec mes amies en bus. J'ai acheté un livre pour ma tante. Ma meilleure amie, Eva, a trouvé une belle robe jaune. On a mangé dans un café. Malheureusement, mes autres amies n'avaient pas d'argent et elles n'ont rien acheté.

(a) Complete the gap in each sentence using a word from the box below.

There are more words than gaps.

with her aunt	by bus	at 8.15
a coffee	a book	a dress
a dress	a belt	nothing

(i) Marie went to town …………… . **(1 mark)**

(ii) She bought ……………………… . **(1 mark)**

(iii) Her best friend found ………… . **(1 mark)**

The diary continues:

> Demain matin je vais rester à la maison avec ma famille. L'après-midi, ma sœur va préparer un repas pour l'anniversaire de ma tante et je vais écouter de la musique dans ma chambre. Le soir, on va donner des cadeaux à ma tante. Elle va être très contente.

(b) Complete the sentences below.

Put a cross [×] in the correct box for each question.

(i) Tomorrow morning Marie is going to …

☐	**A** have a rest.
☐	**B** listen to music.
☐	**C** stay at home.

(ii) in the afternoon her sister is going to …

☐	**A** make a meal.
☐	**B** eat a cake.
☐	**C** sleep.

(2 marks)

(c) Answer the following questions **in English**. You do not need to write in full sentences.

(i) What will they do in the evening? …………………………………………… **(1 mark)**

(ii) How will Marie's aunt feel? ……………………………………………………… **(1 mark)**

(Total for Question 8 = 7 marks)

Practice papers — Had a go ☐ Nearly there ☐ Nailed it! ☐

Future plans

9 Read these comments from an internet forum.

> **Fatima:** Je ne sais pas ce que je vais faire comme travail, mais je vais voyager, car je veux visiter des pays d'Afrique avec mes amies.
>
> **Thomas:** J'ai décidé que je vais me marier à l'avenir car je voudrais avoir quatre enfants. Je voudrais passer mes vacances d'hiver à la montagne au Canada car j'adore la neige.
>
> **Sacha:** L'année prochaine, si j'ai de la chance, j'aimerais aller au lycée où je vais étudier les langues. Je suis forte en anglais, alors je voudrais travailler au Royaume-Uni dans le futur.

Complete the tables **in English**. You do not need to write in full sentences.

	Future plans	Reason why
(a) Fatima		
(b) Thomas		
(c) Sacha		

(6 marks)

Technology

10 Translate the following sentences **into English**.

(a) J'aime les jeux vidéo.

....

(b) Mon frère utilise les réseaux sociaux.

....

(c) Je déteste regarder les films à la télévision.

....

(d) Samedi dernier, j'ai acheté un nouveau portable.

....

(e) Si j'ai le temps, je parle en ligne.

....

(10 marks)

TOTAL FOR PAPER = 50 MARKS

Had a go ☐   Nearly there ☐   Nailed it! ☐

Practice papers

Writing (Foundation)

In the real exam, you will write your answers on the question paper. Here some lines are provided but you may need to write the rest of your answer on your own paper.

Picture-based task

1 Describe the photo. Write four short sentences **in French**.

See this photo in colour

....
....
....
....
....
.... **(8 marks)**

A review

2 Choose either Question 2(a) or Question 2(b).

(a) Write a review of your town / village for a website.	(b) Write a review of your laptop computer for a website.
You **must** include the following points:	You **must** include the following points:
• where the town / village is	• what your laptop looks like
• your opinion of the town / village	• your opinion of your laptop
• when you will next visit the town / village.	• how you will use it this weekend.
Write your answer **in French**. You should aim to write between 40 and 50 words.	Write your answer **in French**. You should aim to write between 40 and 50 words.
(14 marks)	**(14 marks)**

....
....
....
....
....
....

Practice papers

Had a go ☐ Nearly there ☐ Nailed it! ☐

A description

3 Choose either Question 3(a) or Question 3(b).

| (a) Write to your friend about your school.
You **must** include the following points:
• your teachers
• your opinion of your school with reasons
• what you have studied recently
• where you will study next year.
Write your answer **in French**. You should aim to write between 80 and 90 words.
(18 marks) | (b) Write to your friend about your family and friends.
You **must** include the following points:
• your family
• your opinion of your family with reasons
• what you did with your family last week.
• where you will go with your friends next weekend
Write your answer **in French**. You should aim to write between 80 and 90 words.
(18 marks) |

....
....
....
....
....
....

Translation

4 Translate the following five sentences **into French**.

(a) I love exercise.

....

(b) My favourite sport is tennis.

....

(c) I also like to go cycling.

....

(d) Last week I played basketball in the park.

....

(e) I often go to the swimming pool with my best friend.

....

(10 marks)

TOTAL MARKS FOR PAPER = 50

Had a go ☐   Nearly there ☐   Nailed it! ☐

Practice papers

Speaking (Higher)

Pearson Edexcel publishes official Sample Assessment Material on its website. This test has been written to help you practise what you have learned across the four skills and may not be representative of a real exam paper.

Read aloud
My personal world

1 Clara has contributed to a blog about family relationships. Read out the text below.

> Il y a cinq personnes dans ma famille.
> J'ai un frère de huit ans et une sœur qui est plus âgée que moi.
> On fait du sport ensemble le week-end et on s'amuse bien tout le temps.
> Quand je suis triste, mon père m'écoute, et ma mère m'aide souvent avec mes devoirs.

Track 96

Now listen to the recording of two questions related to what you have read.

You are expected to say a few words or a short phrase / sentence in response to each question. One-word answers will not be sufficient to gain full marks.

(12 marks)

Role play

2 **Setting:** At the restaurant

Scenario: You are in a restaurant in France with a friend.

Listen to the recording of the teacher's part. The teacher will play the part of the waiter and will speak first. They will ask questions **in French** and you must answer **in French**. You are expected to say a few words or a short phrase / sentence in response to each prompt. One-word answers will not be sufficient to gain full marks.

> **Task:**
> 1 Say what food you want.
> 2 Ask the price of something on the menu.
> 3 Say what your favourite drink is.
> 4 Say what you will visit tomorrow in the town.
> 5 Ask a question about opening times of the restaurant.

(10 marks)

129

Practice papers

Had a go ☐ Nearly there ☐ Nailed it! ☐

Picture-based task

Picture 1

See this photo in colour

Picture 2

See this photo in colour

3 Describe **ONE** of these pictures. Your description must cover:

- people
- location
- activity. **(8 marks)**

Track 98

Now listen to the recording. You will hear two questions related to each picture above. Answer the two questions related to your chosen picture.

You are expected to say a few words or a short phrase / sentence in response to each question. One-word answers will not be sufficient to gain full marks. **(4 marks)**

You will then move on to a conversation on the broader thematic context of **Travel and tourism**.

Track 99

Play the recording of three questions and choose one to answer. In the real exam, your teacher will ask you more than one question. Practise saying your answer – it should be as full and detailed as possible and could use a variety of tenses. Then listen to the recording of different levels of student answers in the Answer section.

(16 marks)

TOTAL MARKS FOR PAPER = 50

Had a go ☐ Nearly there ☐ Nailed it! ☐

Practice papers

Listening (Higher)

Healthy lifestyles

1 Clara is talking about healthy lifestyles. What does she say?

Listen to the recording and complete the sentences by putting a cross [×] in the correct box for each question.

(a) Clara does sport …
- ☐ **A** once a week.
- ☐ **B** twice a week.
- ☐ **C** twice a day.

(b) Her brother prefers …
- ☐ **A** doing exercise.
- ☐ **B** video games.
- ☐ **C** going cycling.

(c) Last week Clara …
- ☐ **A** went swimming.
- ☐ **B** ate healthy food.
- ☐ **C** played on her computer.

(3 marks)

The environment

2 Hugo is talking about helping the environment in a podcast. What does he say?

Complete the gap in each sentence using a word or phrase from the box below.

There are more words / phrases than gaps.

on foot	by bus	by car
loves	never uses	hates
by train	by bike	by car
nothing	everything	wood
plastic	paper	nothing

(a) When Hugo goes to town, he travels ……………….. .

(b) His mother …………………… her electric car.

(c) When it rains, Hugo travels ……………. to school.

(d) Hugo's brother recycles …………………………….. .

(e) His parents recycle ……………………………………. .

(5 marks)

A new shopping centre

3 Listen to this advert promoting a shopping centre.

What is mentioned?

Listen to the recording and put a cross [×] in each one of the **three** correct boxes.

| ☐ **A** car parks | ☐ **C** having a rest | ☐ **E** children's play area |
| ☐ **B** transport | ☐ **D** places to eat | ☐ **F** supermarkets |

(3 marks)

Free-time activities

4 Clément, Yasmina and Mohamed are talking about their free-time activities. What do they say?

Listen to the recording and complete the sentences by putting a cross [×] in the correct box for each question.

(a) Clément likes going to …
- ☐ **A** town.
- ☐ **B** the beach.
- ☐ **C** visit his mother.

(b) Yasmina goes to the swimming pool …
- ☐ **A** after school.
- ☐ **B** every day.
- ☐ **C** with her friends.

131

(c) From time to time Yasmina goes to the countryside to …

- [ ] **A** go cycling.
- [ ] **B** walk with friends.
- [ ] **C** visit a castle.

(d) On Friday Mohamed is going to …

- [ ] **A** go to a party.
- [ ] **B** celebrate a birthday.
- [ ] **C** buy a present.

(4 marks)

Saving the planet

5 Lucas, Manon and Rachid are talking about the planet. What do they say? Listen to the recording and complete the following table **in English**. You do not need to write in full sentences.

(a)	What Lucas refuses in supermarkets	....
(b)	What Manon thinks the government must do	....
(c)	What Rachid hates to see	....

(3 marks)

School life

6 Thomas is talking about school life. What does he say? Complete the gap in each sentence using a word or phrase from the box below. There are more words / phrases than gaps.

> fair   strict   unfair
> gives lots of homework   doesn't explain things   is never in class
> a different school   travel   tease him

(a) Thomas thinks that the school rules are ....

(b) He dislikes his history teacher because he ....

(c) He is not happy because next year his friends are going to ....

(3 marks)

Holidays

7 Myriam, Théo and Chloé are talking about the advantages and disadvantages of holiday destinations. What do they say? Listen to the podcast and complete the following tables **in English**. You do not need to write in full sentences.

	Advantage	Disadvantage
(a) Myriam		
(b) Théo		
(c) Chloé		

(6 marks)

Getting a job

8 Clara and Mehdi are talking about their views on jobs. What do they say? Listen to the recording and complete the sentences by putting a cross [×] in the correct box for each question.

(a) Clara

(i) Clara's father …

- [ ] **A** earns a lot of money.
- [ ] **B** works in a library.
- [ ] **C** wants to buy his own house.

(ii) Clara find her job …

- [ ] **A** interesting.
- [ ] **B** well paid.
- [ ] **C** boring.

(iii) Clara works …

- [ ] **A** one day a week.
- [ ] **B** with a boss she gets on with.
- [ ] **C** in a little supermarket.

(3 marks)

Had a go ☐ **Nearly there** ☐ **Nailed it!** ☐

Practice papers

(b) Mehdi

(i) Mehdi's ideal job would be …

☐ A abroad.
☐ B a doctor.
☐ C a chemist.

(ii) Mehdi has been …

☐ A studying a foreign language.
☐ B helping others.
☐ C travelling in Africa.

(iii) Mehdi thinks that …

☐ A it's sad when people don't like their job.
☐ B it's not essential to be well paid.
☐ C he will succeed.

(3 marks)
(Total for Question 8 = 6 marks)

Helping others

9 (a) Fatima is talking about helping others. What does she say?

Listen to the podcast and put a cross [×] in each one of the **three** correct boxes.

☐	A	She has been volunteering with friends for two years.
☐	B	She has been helping young and old people.
☐	C	They recently organised a visit to a zoo.
☐	D	She would like to organise a visit to a zoo.
☐	E	She is going to work for a charity.
☐	F	She has recently helped animals in danger.

(3 marks)

(b) You also hear this report on helping others in France and abroad.

Listen to the recording and answer the following questions **in English**.

You do not need to write in full sentences.

(i) Name one thing that France respects ……………………………………………………………

(ii) What has just been set up? ……………………………………………………………………

(iii) What has been a success in Paris? ……………………………………………………………

(iv) What will take place next year? ………………………………………………………………

(4 marks)
(Total for Question 9 = 7 marks)

Dictation

10 You are going to hear someone talking about his area.

Sentences 1–2: write down the missing words in the gaps provided. In each gap, you will write one word **in French**.

Example: Ma <u>région</u> est <u>dans</u> le <u>sud</u> de la France.

1 Dans ma ………………., il y a une ……… et un …………………….. .

2 Les touristes ………… …………….. et se …………………………… .

Sentences 3–6: write down the full sentences that you hear in the spaces provided, **in French**.

Example: <u>J'aime les cafés, les restaurants et les magasins</u>.

3 ………………………………………………………………………………………………. .

4 ………………………………………………………………………………………………. .

5 ………………………………………………………………………………………………. .

6 ………………………………………………………………………………………………. .

(10 marks)

TOTAL MARKS FOR PAPER = 50

Reading (Higher)

School trips

1 Read the email that Hugo wrote to his French friend.

> Salut!
> J'aime mon collège car je m'entends bien avec les élèves et les professeurs et on fait beaucoup de voyages scolaires. Le mois dernier, je suis allé au stade dans une grande ville avec ma classe et on a participé à une journée de sport. Moi, j'ai joué au foot et mon équipe a gagné. C'était passionnant!
> L'année prochaine, nous allons en France pour regarder un match de basket à Paris.
> Tu fais des visites scolaires?
> Hugo

Complete the gap in each sentence using a word from the box below.

There are more words than gaps.

headteacher	friends	students
lost	won	drew
next month	next year	in March

(a) Hugo gets on well with the teachers and ………………………… .

(b) At the sports day, his team ……………………………………... .

(c) He is going to France ……………………………………………… . **(3 marks)**

Future plans

2 Read Mathis's blog about the future.

> Je m'appelle Mathis et j'ai commencé à penser à mon avenir. J'ai toujours voulu devenir professeur, mais la formation est très longue et quand je vois les jeunes de mon quartier qui ne respectent pas la planète, j'ai changé d'avis.
> J'ai l'intention de trouver un petit travail car j'ai besoin de l'argent pour acheter des vêtements, des jeux vidéo et peut-être un nouveau portable, mais plus tard, je voudrais trouver un métier intéressant. Maintenant je crois que je voudrais être **comptable**, comme ma mère qui travaille dans une banque, parce que j'aime les maths.

(a) Complete the sentences below.

Put a cross [×] in the correct box for each question.

(i) Mathis has started to think about …
- ☐ A his school.
- ☐ B his future.
- ☐ C his friends.

(ii) He thinks that teachers …
- ☐ A work long hours.
- ☐ B have a long training period.
- ☐ C like children.

(iii) He intends to …
- ☐ A get a part-time job.
- ☐ B save the planet.
- ☐ C sell mobile phones.

(iv) He would like to …
- ☐ A find an interesting job.
- ☐ B find a well-paid job.
- ☐ C work with children.

Had a go ☐ **Nearly there** ☐ **Nailed it!** ☐

Practice papers

(b) Which of these is the best translation for the word *comptable*?

Put a cross [×] in the correct box.

☐ **A** teacher ☐ **B** baker ☐ **C** accountant

(5 marks)

A diary entry

3 Marie writes in her diary.

> Ce matin à huit heures et demie, je suis allée en ville avec mes amies en bus. J'ai acheté un livre pour ma tante. Ma meilleure amie, Eva, a trouvé une belle robe jaune. On a mangé dans un café. Malheureusement, mes autres amies n'avaient pas d'argent et elles n'ont rien acheté.

(a) Complete the gap in each sentence using a word from the box below.

There are more words than gaps.

with her aunt	by bus	at 8.15
a coffee	a book	a dress
a dress	a belt	nothing

(i) Marie went to town .... **(1 mark)**

(ii) She bought .... **(1 mark)**

(iii) Her best friend found .... **(1 mark)**

The diary continues:

> Demain matin je vais rester à la maison avec ma famille. L'après-midi, ma sœur va préparer un repas pour l'anniversaire de ma tante et je vais écouter de la musique dans ma chambre. Le soir, on va donner des cadeaux à ma tante. Elle va être très contente.

(b) Complete the sentences below.

Put a cross [×] in the correct box for each question.

(i) Tomorrow morning Marie is going to …

☐ **A** have a rest.
☐ **B** listen to music.
☐ **C** stay at home.

(ii) In the afternoon her sister is going to …

☐ **A** make a meal.
☐ **B** eat a cake.
☐ **C** sleep.

(2 marks)

(c) Answer the following questions **in English**. You do not need to write in full sentences.

(i) What will they do in the evening? .... **(1 mark)**

(ii) How will Marie's aunt feel? .... **(1 mark)**

(Total for Question 3 = 7 marks)

Celebrity culture

4 Read Clara's email to Luis.

> ✉
>
> Mon acteur préféré, c'est Michel Marsaud* et je le suis sur les réseaux sociaux. Il a du talent, il est beau et sympa, et je l'adore! Selon ma mère, il est parfait! Il sera dans ma ville dimanche prochain car il visitera le nouveau cinéma avec sa femme. Michel sait bien danser, et il chante aussi! Je le trouve très *doué*! Je voudrais y aller et j'ai de la chance parce que j'ai déjà acheté un billet. Je suis contente.

*fictional actor

135

(a) Answer the following questions **in English**. You do not need to write in full sentences.

(i) What does Clara's mother think of Michel? .... **(1 mark)**

(ii) When does Clara say that she is lucky? .... **(1 mark)**

(b) Which of these is the best translation of the word *doué*?

Put a cross [×] in the correct box.

| ☐ A rich | ☐ B gifted | ☐ C busy |

(Total for Question 4 = 3 marks)

Holidays

5 Jules and Yanis have written blogs about their holidays.

> Je m'appelle Jules. Il y a deux ans, j'ai passé les meilleures vacances de ma vie. On est allés en Algérie et c'était génial. Le premier jour, après avoir visité une belle île, on a essayé des sports extrêmes et c'était passionnant. À la fin des vacances, j'ai commencé à pleurer car je ne voulais pas rentrer chez moi!

(a) What does Jules say about his holidays?

Put a cross [×] next to each one of the **three** correct statements.

☐	A	Jules went to Algeria last year.
☐	B	He visited an island on the first day of his holidays.
☐	C	He doesn't like extreme sports.
☐	D	He didn't enjoy his holidays much.
☐	E	He cried on the last day.
☐	F	He didn't want to go home.

(3 marks)

> Salut! C'est Yanis. Je viens de rentrer de vacances difficiles avec mon oncle au Canada. D'abord, le vol a été beaucoup trop long et il a fait vraiment mauvais, alors j'ai eu très peur! Ensuite, en route pour notre hôtel, mon oncle a perdu sa valise et il a dû acheter de nouveaux vêtements.

(b) What does Yanis say about his holidays?

Complete the tables **in English**. You do not need to write in full sentences.

(i) The flight	
(ii) Yanis's feelings during the flight	
(iii) Where a suitcase went missing	
(iv) What Yanis's uncle had to do	

(4 marks)

(Total for Question 5 = 7 marks)

Moving house

6 Read this text which Louis has written for a school project.

> Lorsque j'étais plus jeune, j'habitais dans la banlieue de Paris où il y avait beaucoup de violence. Il n'y avait ni fleurs ni arbres et tout le monde semblait triste. C'était vraiment difficile d'y habiter.
>
> Aujourd'hui, je vis dans un bel appartement dans un village où le paysage est très beau. J'ai toujours voulu habiter ailleurs qu'en banlieue et maintenant, je suis heureux, surtout qu'il n'y a presque pas de bruit et ma famille sourit beaucoup!

Had a go ☐ **Nearly there** ☐ **Nailed it!** ☐

Practice papers

(a) What does Louis say?

Put a cross [×] next to each one of the **two** correct statements.

☐	**A** He didn't use to like living in the suburbs.
☐	**B** There were lots of flowers and trees where he used to live.
☐	**C** He likes the landscape where he now lives.
☐	**D** There's a little too much noise where he lives now.

(2 marks)

Louis's text continues.

> Mon père, qui travaillait comme policier à Paris, n'avait pas confiance en lui, alors il a décidé de changer de métier. Après avoir fait une formation de six mois, il a enfin réussi à trouver du travail dans un gymnase. C'est bien car il a toujours été sportif et il adore être actif. Il est devenu moins stressé et maintenant, il est plus heureux. Il vient de créer sa propre entreprise comme **entraîneur*** professionnel et nous sommes vraiment fiers de lui!

entraîneur – trainer

(b) Complete the tables **in English**. You do not need to write in full sentences.

(i) How Louis's father used to be	
(ii) How long he trained for	
(iii) How they feel about Louis's father	

(3 marks)

(Total for Question 6 = 5 marks)

A film festival

7 Read this online article about a film festival.

> Le festival de films francophones se passe cette année à Montréal* au Canada. Ceux qui aiment le cinéma peuvent regarder des films célèbres pendant deux semaines à des prix réduits, et on peut décider le film qui gagne le grand prix.
>
> Le festival commence le 12 juillet et tous les soirs, il y a un concert où on peut écouter de la musique moderne. Cette année, il y aura plus de cinquante groupes, et le chanteur canadien Julien sera là. On espère qu'il fera beau car les concerts sont dehors!
>
> Si vous voulez participer au festival, vous pouvez vous présenter à l'office de tourisme ou y envoyer un e-mail. Les billets sont disponibles maintenant, alors bonne chance!

Montréal – a French-speaking city in Canada

(a) Complete the sentences below.

Put a cross [×] in the correct box for each question.

(i) The film festival lasts ...

☐	**A** 2 weeks.
☐	**B** a year.
☐	**C** 12 days.

(ii) The price of tickets ...

☐	**A** is high.
☐	**B** is reduced.
☐	**C** is higher than last year.

(iii) This year there will be ...

☐	**A** only Canadian singers.
☐	**B** more than 50 groups.
☐	**C** 50 films to watch.

(3 marks)

(b) Answer the following questions **in English**. You do not need to write in full sentences.

(i) Why do they hope for warm weather? ....

(ii) When are the tickets available? ....

(2 marks)

(Total for Question 7 = 5 marks)

Practice papers

Had a go ☐ Nearly there ☐ Nailed it! ☐

A magazine article

8 Read this article, written by Luis, for a Belgian magazine.

> Salut, tout le monde !
> Un groupe d'adolescents de notre ville a décidé de devenir plus sains. On a commencé à faire attention à ce qu'on mange et ce qu'on boit, et on a aussi réussi à améliorer notre santé en faisant plus d'exercice physique.
> Avant, je mangeais beaucoup de fast-food et je détestais les fruits et les légumes. Je me sentais souvent inquiet et un peu malade, vu que je passais trop de temps chez moi à regarder un écran. Maintenant, j'évite la nourriture qui est mauvaise pour la santé, je cours chaque matin et je suis plus actif. Mes copains disent que je suis moins stressé et plus heureux.
> Dès demain, nous allons essayer d'aider les autres à suivre un régime sain et d'améliorer la forme de nos familles. Nous allons aussi participer à une émission qui va expliquer le lien scientifique entre la nourriture malsaine et la maladie.

Answer the following questions **in English**. You do not need to write in full sentences.

(a) Name one thing that the group of teenagers started to do.

....

(b) Why was Luis often anxious and ill?

....

(c) What does he now do every morning?

....

(d) Name one thing the group is going to try to do.

....

(e) What is the purpose of the programme which they are participating in?

....

(5 marks)

Helping other

9 Translate the following paragraph **into English**.

> J'aide souvent les gens de mon quartier. Plus tard, je voudrais étudier le droit. Mes copains et moi pensons que l'égalité est importante. J'ai déjà donné de l'argent aux pauvres qui habitent dans ma rue. L'année prochaine, je travaillerai pour une association qui aide les personnes âgées.

....
....
....
....
....
....
....

(10 marks)

TOTAL FOR PAPER = 50 MARKS

Had a go ☐ Nearly there ☐ Nailed it! ☐

Practice papers

Writing (Higher)

In the real exam, you will write your answers on the question paper. Here some lines are provided but you may need to write the rest of your answer on your own paper.

A description

1 Choose either Question 1(a) or Question 1(b).

| (a) Write to your friend about your school

You **must** include the following points:
• your teachers
• your opinion of your school with reasons
• what you have studied recently
• where you will study next year.

Write your answer **in French**. You should aim to write between 80 and 90 words.

(18 marks) | (b) Write to your friend about your family and friends

You **must** include the following points:
• your family
• your opinion of your family with reasons
• what you did with your family last week
• where you will go with your friends next weekend.

Write your answer **in French**. You should aim to write between 80 and 90 words.

(18 marks) |

....
....
....
....
....
....
....
....
....

An opinion

2 Choose either Question 2(a) or 2(b).

| (a) Write about holidays for an online magazine.

You **must** include the following points:
• what makes a good holiday
• the pros and cons of going on holiday abroad
• what activities you did on holiday last year
• where you will go on holiday next year.

Write your answer **in French**. You should aim to write between 130 and 150 words.

(22 marks) | (b) Write about technology for an online magazine.

You **must** include the following points:
• what makes a good social media site
• the pros and cons of technology
• what activities you did online last week
• where you will use the internet in the future.

Write your answer **in French**. You should aim to write between 130 and 150 words.

(22 marks) |

Practice papers

Had a go ☐ Nearly there ☐ Nailed it! ☐

....
....
....
....
....
....
....
....
....
....
....
....
....

Translation

3 Translate the paragraph **into French**.

> I like going shopping in town. My sister often comes with me. I always travel by bus or by train. Last month I bought a skirt and some trainers online. My friends are going to visit a new shopping centre next weekend because they want to find a present for my birthday.

....
....
....
....
....
....
....
....

(10 marks)

TOTAL MARKS FOR PAPER = 50

Answers

The answers to the Speaking and Writing activities below are sample answers – there are many ways you could answer these questions.

1. Physical descriptions

Reading

1

	Who ...	Ana	Lucas	Camille
(a)	has ginger hair?			×
(b)	has a friend with blue eyes?			×
(c)	is quite tall?			×
(d)	has a friend who wears glasses?		×	
(e)	has a smaller friend?	×		
(f)	is very tall?	×		

Listening

2 1 J'ai **les** yeux **verts**.
   2 Mon amie a les **cheveux** noirs et **frisés**.
   3 Elle **est** très **grande** et **drôle**.
   4 Je la trouve amusante.
   5 Je suis assez calme.
   6 On dit que je suis travailleur.

2. Character descriptions

Speaking

1 Sample answers:
   1 Ma meilleure amie, qui s'appelle Fatima, est très travailleuse et assez patiente. Elle est sérieuse de temps en temps mais elle n'est jamais triste.
   2 Quand j'étais plus jeune, j'étais vraiment sportif car je jouais au foot et je faisais de la natation. J'étais plus calme et assez heureux.
   3 Je me fais du souci pour mon ami Luke parce qu'à mon avis, il n'est pas travailleur et il est souvent triste. Je le trouve stressé.
   4 Le sport m'intéresse beaucoup parce que je suis très actif.

Listening

2 (a) B (b) C (c) A

3. Friends

Speaking

1 Read aloud text

Reading

2 (a) at a party, two weeks ago
   (b) fun / funny / amusing
   (c) shopping / bought things
   (d) that the friendship will last a long time, because they have the same tastes

4. Family

Listening

1 (a) B (b) C (c) A (d) B

Writing

2 (a) J'adore ma famille.
   (b) Mon père est très patient.
   (c) Ma mère m'écoute beaucoup.
   (d) Je suis en vacances avec ma tante.
   (e) Hier, je suis allé(e) à la plage avec mes frères.

5. Relationships

Reading

1 A D F

Speaking

2 Sample answers:
Il y a quatre jeunes amis. Un garçon a les cheveux blonds et l'autre garçon a les cheveux noirs. Les filles ont les cheveux longs et une fille porte une chemise jaune. Ils sont dans la rue devant une maison et je pense qu'il fait beau car ils ne portent pas de pulls. Ils utilisent des portables et selon moi, ils sont contents parce qu'ils sourient. Je pense qu'ils s'entendent bien.
(a) J'aime jouer au foot avec mes amis car je suis sportif / sportive.
(b) Oui. Ma meilleure amie s'appelle Sarah et elle est très sympa.

6. Helping friends with problems

Listening

1 A B D
2 1 J'aide **beaucoup** mon **ami**.
   2 Mon ami ne **mange** pas **assez**.
   3 Maintenant il **est** en **forme**.
   4 J'écoute ses soucis.
   5 Il y a une crise.
   6 Mon meilleur ami est souvent déprimé.

7. When I was younger

Speaking

1 (a) swimming (b) in a small flat (c) cooking

Conversation

2 Sample answers:
   (a) Quand j'étais plus jeune, j'allais en vacances au Canada avec ma famille. On faisait des sports d'hiver à la montagne et je trouvais ça amusant. Le soir, on allait manger dans un restaurant près d'un lac. Les repas étaient délicieux et la vue était extraordinaire. Cependant, maintenant, on va en France et je n'aime pas ça parce que c'est nul. Je voudrais retourner au Canada.
   (b) Quand j'étais plus jeune, je faisais des achats en ville le samedi avec ma mère et mes amies. J'aimais aussi chanter et danser car j'étais vraiment active. Cependant, maintenant, je préfère jouer sur mon ordinateur et télécharger de la musique sur mon portable.

8. Identity

Writing

1 Sample answer:
Je suis assez sportif et j'aime presque tous les sports, mais je n'aime pas le football. Je pense que je suis sérieux. Ma passion, c'est la lecture, et je lis tous les jours. On dit que je suis travailleur et aussi sympa parce que je fais toujours mes devoirs et j'aime aider les autres.
Récemment, je suis allé en ville où j'ai acheté beaucoup de livres et le week-end dernier, j'ai fait du vélo avec mes amis.
À l'avenir, je voudrais devenir professeur car je pense qu'il est important d'aider les enfants.

Speaking

2 Sample answer:
   (a) Je pense que je suis assez patient(e). On dit que je suis toujours amusant(e). Mes amis disent que je ne suis pas sportif / sportive mais ils ont tort parce que j'adore faire de la natation.
   (b) Je veux aider les autres. Alors je voudrais devenir médecin. Je voudrais aussi voyager pour voir d'autres cultures différentes. Je rêve de visiter l'Afrique.

9. Everyday life

Writing

1 Sample answer:

Je me lève à sept heures et demie tous des jours. Avant de quitter la maison, je prends le petit-déjeuner, je regarde la télé ou j'envoie des textos à mes amis. Après être arrivé au collège, j'ai toujours quatre cours avant le déjeuner. Normalement, je mange à la cantine et les repas sont excellents. Je rentre chez moi après le dernier cours.

Ma région est assez agréable, mais je la trouve un peu ennuyeuse car il n'y a pas assez de magasins.

Samedi dernier, je suis allé en ville avec mon frère et nous avons acheté un cadeau pour l'anniversaire de mon père.

À l'avenir, je voudrais habiter à l'étranger, peut-être dans le sud de la France parce qu'il y fait chaud.

Reading

2 My life is quite simple. After spending a tiring day at school, I return home, really tired. Previously I used to do my homework immediately, but now I prefer to go out with some friends. My town isn't interesting, so I dream of living somewhere else. I think that I'll look for a job because I need more money.

10. Meals at home

Writing

1 Sample answer:

Chez moi, je ne prends jamais de petit-déjeuner car je n'ai pas faim le matin, mais le soir, j'aime manger des pâtes ou du riz. À mon avis mon père prépare des repas délicieux et je les trouve vraiment super.

Hier, nous avons mangé du poisson avec des frites, mais ma mère nous a dit que c'était malsain.

Demain nous allons manger un repas spécial car ce sera l'anniversaire de ma sœur. Moi, je préparerai un gros gâteau au chocolat et on s'amusera bien.

Listening

2 (a) B (b) C (c) C (d) A

11. Celebrations

Writing

1 Sample answers:
1. Il y a quatre personnes.
2. Je vois un cadeau.
3. La fille a 18 ans.
4. Il y a un gâteau.

Reading

2 (a) Toni's elder / older sister
(b) a designer / branded dress
(c) a hat
(d) Her sister has been invited to a wedding / marriage. / Her sister wants one.

12. Food and drink

Writing

1 Sample answer:

Pour le petit-déjeuner, normalement, je prends un jus de fruit car je n'ai pas faim, mais le week-end, j'aime bien manger des œufs. Ce que j'aime le plus, c'est la viande avec des frites parce que j'adore le goût. L'année dernière, je suis allé en vacances au Canada avec ma famille. On a essayé la cuisine de la région et je l'ai trouvée super car on mange beaucoup de plats sucrés, au Canada!

À l'avenir, je voudrais manger des repas végétariens car on dit qu'ils sont bons pour la santé et je pense qu'il est important d'être en forme.

Speaking

2 Sample answer:

Example of a grades 2–4 answer: Je préfère boire de l'eau car c'est sain. De temps en temps, j'aime aussi boire du lait, mais je déteste le thé car ce n'est pas bon.

 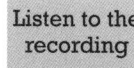

Listen to the recording

Example of a grades 5–6 or 7 answer: Je préfère boire de l'eau car c'est sain. De temps en temps, j'aime aussi boire du lait, mais je déteste le thé car ce n'est pas bon. Récemment, j'ai décidé de ne plus boire de chocolat chaud car on dit que c'est mauvais pour la santé, même si c'est vraiment délicieux. Je ne boirai jamais de café car je n'aime pas le goût.

13. Healthy diets

Listening

1 1 J'aime les **glaces**, les **gâteaux** et les **pêches**.
2 Mes **fruits** préférés sont les **pommes** et les **framboises**.
3 J'aime aussi tous les légumes.
4 J'évite le poisson et les frites.
5 Je dois boire plus d'eau.
6 Je commande toujours de la viande.

Reading

2 A C E

14. Sport and exercise

Speaking

1 Sample answer:
1 Bonjour. Je peux vous aider?
Je voudrais jouer au tennis.
Très bien.
2 C'est pour combien de personnes?
C'est pour deux personnes.
D'accord.
3 Quelles activités allez-vous faire plus tard?
Je vais jouer au handball ce soir.
C'est intéressant.
4 Vous avez une question?
Vous fermez à quelle heure?
Vingt heures.
5 Vous avez une autre question?
C'est combien?
Vingt-cinq euros.

Listen to the recording

Writing

2 Sample answer:

Mon gymnase est au centre-ville, près de ma maison, et je vais au gymnase le samedi avec mes amis. J'adore le gymnase car on peut faire de l'exercice et c'est important pour la forme. Je vais aussi aller au gymnase vendredi prochain.

15. Physical wellbeing

Speaking

1 Sample answers for follow-on questions:
(a) J'aime boire du café.
(b) Le sport, c'est amusant.

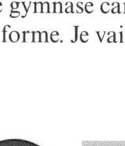
Listen to the recording

Reading

2 (a) improve his fitness / have sporting success
(b) individual / one you can play / do alone
(c) train (at a sports club)
(d) B

16. Mental wellbeing

Speaking

Sample answers:
(a) Selon moi, la santé mentale est aussi importante que la santé physique, car beaucoup de jeunes sont stressés par la pression causée par les examens ou les dangers en ligne. Le harcèlement est terrible et mon meilleur copain a pleuré la semaine dernière parce qu'on l'a menacé en ligne.
(b) Beaucoup de personnes ont des problèmes mentaux et il y a une vraie crise. Je pense que quelquefois, on trouve difficile de s'intégrer à la société. On passe trop de temps devant un écran

Listen to the recording

et je pense qu'il faut combattre les problèmes causés par Internet.

Writing

2   (a) Je suis triste.
    (b) Mon ami(e) ne peut pas dormir.
    (c) La santé mentale est importante.
    (d) Je pense que j'ai trop d'examens et je suis stressé(e).
    (e) La semaine dernière, j'ai commencé à faire plus de sport pour aider ma santé mentale.

17. Feeling unwell

Writing

1   Sample answers:
    Il y a trois personnes.
    Ils sont malades.
    La fille porte un chapeau jaune
    Ils sont dans une maison.

Reading

2   C D F

18. Equality and sporting role models

Writing

1   (a) L'égalité est très importante.
    (b) Je respecte beaucoup de célébrités sportives.
    (c) Je pense que je peux aider les gens.
    (d) Je ne veux pas être riche ou célèbre.
    (e) La semaine dernière, j'ai regardé mon modèle à la télévision.

Listening

2   B D F

19. Sporting events

Writing

1   Sample answers:
    Il y a quatre personnes.
    Ils regardent un match de football.
    Je vois une télévision.
    Un homme porte un pull bleu.

Reading

2   I love watching sports on TV and I often go to sporting events. Recently, my friend invited me to watch the Tour de France since she knew that we would have fun. I found the competition interesting, but it rained all day. Next year, I am going to watch a professional football match. After the bad weather we had for the cycling, I hope that it will be better weather for the football!

20. Me and my mobile

Speaking

1   Sample answer:
Il y a trois jeunes dans la rue – deux garçons et seulement une fille. Ils regardent le portable de la fille au centre de la photo et je pense qu'il y a une surprise sur son portable. Il semble qu'ils ont peut-être vu quelque chose d'étonnant. Un garçon et la fille portent une chemise et l'autre garçon porte une veste. À mon avis, les trois personnes sont des étudiants car ils portent des sacs. Je dirais qu'ils sont des amis.
(a) J'aime envoyer des messages à mes copains.
(b) Hier, j'ai téléchargé de la musique et j'ai regardé un film.

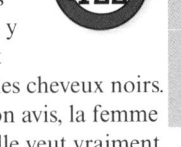

Reading

2   (a) Jade (b) Alex (c) Jade (d) Toni (e) Alex (f) Toni

21. Social media

Speaking

1   Sample answers:
    (a) J'aime les réseaux sociaux car on peut parler avec ses amis et je trouve ça génial. Pourtant, il y a des risques et on doit protéger son identité.
    (b) Je passe trois heures en ligne chaque jour. Ma mère a dit que je dois essayer de passer moins de temps sur Internet car c'est mauvais pour la santé et les yeux.

Reading

2   (a) essential in his daily life
    (b) bullying / harassment; cybercrimes / criminality
    (c) an interesting video about helping the poor in Madagascar
    (d) smile

22. The internet

Listening

1   1 Mon **père** déteste **Internet**.
    2 En ligne, j'**écoute** de la musique **américaine**.
    3 J'aime **acheter** des **bottes** chères.
    4 Je partage mes photos.
    5 On peut regarder des films.
    6 Il y a des dangers.

Writing

2   Sample answer:
Mon ordinateur portable est plus grand que mon portable et je l'aime beaucoup parce que c'est un cadeau de ma mère. J'aime aussi la couleur et la marque.
La semaine prochaine, je vais faire mon travail scolaire en ligne, mais le week-end je vais regarder un film sur mon ordinateur et ça va être génial. (Grade 4)

23. Computer games

Speaking

1   Sample answer:
Sur la photo il y a deux jeunes gens qui participent aux jeux en ligne. Il y a une femme et un homme. Ils sont dans la maison. Tous les deux ont les cheveux noirs. La femme porte des lunettes. À mon avis, la femme est en train de perdre le jeu, mais elle veut vraiment gagner. Il me semble qu'ils s'amusent bien.
(a) J'aime faire des jeux en ligne car je trouve que c'est un moyen efficace de combattre le stress de ma vie quotidienne.
(b) Récemment j'ai participé à un match de football en ligne avec mes copains. C'était génial et on s'est bien amusés.

Reading

2   (a) B (b) A (c) B (d) A

24. Pros and cons of technology

Listening

1   (a) change password every month
    (b) identity theft
    (c) cannot go online after 8 pm

Reading

2   A D F

25. Hobbies

Writing

1   Sample answer:
Après une semaine au collège, les jeunes font souvent des sports différents pour s'amuser. Aussi, ils font du théâtre ou jouent à des jeux vidéo en ligne avec des amis, par exemple. Je préfère être actif, alors je fais beaucoup de sport. Mon sport préféré est le football parce que je suis fort au foot!

143

Le week-end dernier, je suis allé en ville avec mon meilleur ami et nous avons vu un film au cinéma. Selon moi, c'était étonnant parce que j'ai aimé tous les acteurs!

La semaine prochaine, je vais faire du cheval avec mes sœurs et nous allons aller au bord de la mer où je vais faire la natation.

Reading
2 (a) A (b) B (c) A (d) C

26. Music and dance

Writing
1 Sample answer:
Il y a six personnes.
Ils dansent.
Un homme joue d'un instrument.
Je vois trois jeunes femmes.

Speaking
2 Sample answers:
1 Je peux vous aider?
   Je voudrais aller à un concert de musique pop.
2 Très bien. Vous avez une question?
   C'est combien?
3 Cinquante euros. C'est votre ami qui paie?
   Non, je paie.
4 Très bien. Où irez-vous après le concert?
   J'irai au restaurant avec mon ami.
5 Vous avez une autre question?
   Le concert finit à quelle heure?
   Vingt-deux heures.

27. Arranging to go out

Speaking
1 Read aloud text

Reading
2 (a) by his best friend
    (b) near Hugo's house
    (c) stay at home
    (d) photos
    (e) a crowd

28. Reading

Writing
1 (a) J'adore lire / la lecture.
    (b) Ma sœur lit tous les jours si elle a le temps.
    (c) Je pense que les livres sont intéressants.
    (d) La semaine dernière j'ai acheté un journal en ville.
    (e) Je veux lire plus souvent.

Reading
2 C D F

29. Television

Reading
1 (a) A (b) A (c) C

Listening
2 1 act / actor in a soap opera / drama series
   2 the news
   3 sports programmes

30. Going to the cinema

Speaking
1 Sample answers:
1 Bonjour. Je peux vous aider?
   Je voudrais voir un film d'action.
2 Très bien. Vous avez une question?
   Quel est le prix pour un étudiant?
   Ça coûte huit euros pour un étudiant.
3 Pourquoi aimez-vous aller au cinéma?
   On peut voir de nouveaux films.
4 Vous avez vu un film, récemment?
   Samedi dernier, j'ai vu une comédie.
5 Intéressant. Vous avez une autre question?
   Est-ce qu'on peut acheter un café au cinéma?
   Bien sûr.

Writing
2 Sample answer:
Quand je sors avec mes copains, on va souvent au centre-ville où on peut acheter des vêtements ou aller au cinéma qui se trouve près de chez moi. Le cinéma est grand et j'aime ça car on peut y voir beaucoup de films différents comme des films d'action ou des comédies. Je préfère les films qui me font sourire.
Le week-end dernier, je suis allé en ville où j'ai acheté un cadeau pour l'anniversaire de ma mère. C'était génial parce que je lui ai acheté une robe qui était très chère !
Le week-end prochain, je vais voir un documentaire.

31. Celebrity culture

Listening
1 (a) forget his problems
    (b) fashion
    (c) rich

Reading
2 (a) I like watching / to watch celebrities on TV.
    (b) My favourite actor is very funny.
    (c) If I have time, I read articles on singers.
    (d) Last week I went to a concert.
    (e) My parents are never interested in famous people.

32. Role models

Listening
1 C E F

Writing
2 J'aime beaucoup chanter. Mon artiste préférée est célèbre en France et l'année dernière, je suis allé la voir en concert. C'était la meilleure soirée de ma vie! Elle m'inspire car elle est sympa et patiente. Je vais écouter sa nouvelle chanson en ligne la semaine prochaine et j'espère que ce sera génial.

33. Places in town

Reading
1 (a) a library or a gym
    (b) a new swimming pool has just been built
    (c) abroad

Writing
2 Sample answer:
Selon moi, une bonne ville devrait avoir un grand centre commercial où on peut faire les magasins et aussi un centre sportif pour ceux qui aiment le sport.
Ma ville est trop petite et il n'y a pas assez d'activités sportives disponibles. Cependant, ma ville est très belle, les rues sont propres et j'adore les arbres qu'on voit partout dans la région. Récemment, j'ai passé deux heures au centre-ville avec ma famille et c'était vraiment génial. Après avoir pris un repas excellent dans un petit café, nous sommes allés au musée d'art où on a pu admirer de beaux tableaux.
À l'avenir, je voudrais habiter dans une plus grande ville comme Paris parce qu'il y a beaucoup de choses à faire. Je trouverai un emploi là-bas et j'achèterai un appartement près de la rivière. Ce sera vraiment passionnant!

34. Things to do

Reading
1 (a) B (b) A (c) B

Writing
2 (a) J'adore le sport.
    (b) J'aime faire les magasins en ville.
    (c) Dans mon quartier on peut visiter le marché.
    (d) Hier j'ai fait du vélo avec mes amis.
    (e) Jeudi je vais voir un film avec ma sœur et ma tante.

35. Shopping

Listening
1.
   1. Ma mère **va** aux **magasins**.
   2. Elle **aime** acheter des **shorts**.
   3. **J'achète** une **veste**.
   4. J'adore les baskets.
   5. Mon frère préfère les pantalons.
   6. Je veux une nouvelle chemise.

Speaking
2. Sample answers:
   1. Bonjour, je peux vous aider?
      Je voudrais acheter un pull.
   2. Ah oui, c'est quelle taille?
      Je fais une taille moyenne.
   3. D'accord. Vous avez une question?
      C'est combien, le pull?
      Ça coûte quinze euros.
   4. Vous allez faire les magasins, demain?
      Oui, demain, je vais acheter un sac.
   5. Ah. Vous avez une autre question?
      Le magasin ferme à quelle heure?
      Nous fermons à dix-huit heures.

36. Transport

Speaking
1. Sample answer:
Sur la photo, je peux voir quatre personnes. La fille, qui a les cheveux blonds, parle à deux garçons qui sont assis dans un train. Les deux garçons ont les cheveux courts. Un garçon écoute de la musique et l'autre porte un pull et il a un sac. Ils portent des baskets. Au fond, il y a aussi un homme plus âgé qui est assis derrière les jeunes. Il a un livre. Je pense que la fille et les garçons sont des amis, mais ils ne connaissent pas l'autre homme.
(a) J'aime les trains car ils sont rapides.
(b) Je vais en ville avec mes amis en bus.

Listening
2. Myriam
   Disadvantage: (many) delays
   Advantage: not dangerous
   Théo
   Advantage: good for the environment
   Disadvantage: tiring

37. Travel and buying tickets

Speaking
1. Sample answers:
   1. Bonjour, Je peux vous aider?
      Je veux un aller-retour pour Paris.
   2. Pas de problème. Avec qui voyagez-vous?
      Je voyage avec mes amis.
   3. Très bien. Quel est votre moyen de transport préféré?
      Je préfère la voiture.
   4. Intéressant. Que pensez-vous du café à la gare?
      Il est excellent.
   5. D'accord! Vous avez une question pour moi?
      Le train part à quelle heure?
      Le train part à deux heures.

Reading
2. A D F

38. My region – good and bad

Speaking
1. Sample answer:
J'aime ma région parce qu'il y a beaucoup de choses à faire et à voir. Par exemple, on peut visiter le vieux château qui attire les touristes, surtout en été quand il fait beau. Je suis allé au château avec ma tante l'année dernière et c'était vraiment intéressant. Cependant, il y a trop de bruit au centre-ville et la pollution est un problème sérieux. Je pense qu'on devrait améliorer la ville et je dirais qu'il faut avoir plus d'espaces verts.

Reading
2. (a) A (b) C (c) A

39. My area in the past

Listening
1. (a) B (b) A (c) B

Reading
2. (a) dirtier / less clean **(1)** bottles in street(s) **(1)**
   (b) safe / less crime and violence / no need to be afraid
   (c) too much pollution

40. Town or country

Listening
1. Lola: advantage: healthier; disadvantage: nothing for young people to do
   Mohamed: advantage: can see flowers and trees; disadvantage: cannot shop easily
   Sarah: advantage: can do lots of outdoor activities; disadvantage: not enough buses

Writing
2. Sample answers:
   Il y a quatre personnes.
   Je vois une famille.
   C'est à la campagne.
   La femme prépare un repas.

41. During the holidays

Reading
1. A B F

Writing
2. L'année dernière, je suis allé(e) en Martinique avec ma famille. J'ai passé des heures sur la plage où j'ai joué au football et j'ai regardé les bateaux. Il faisait beau, donc on était dehors tout le temps. J'aime aller à l'étranger car j'adore découvrir des cultures différentes et essayer de nouveaux plats. L'année prochaine, en juillet, nous allons visiter le Canada.

42. Abroad

Reading
1. (a) Nathan (b) Mathis (c) Mathis (d) Fatima (e) Nathan (f) Fatima

Writing
2. Sample answer:
Selon moi, les vacances sont très importantes car il faut oublier les problèmes de la vie quotidienne de temps en temps! J'aime découvrir d'autres pays et de goûter les plats traditionnels de chaque pays.
J'ai déjà passé beaucoup de temps à l'étranger, mais mon endroit préféré est la France. J'y vais souvent et j'aime ce pays car les gens sont sympas et en été, il fait toujours beau et chaud, surtout dans le sud.
L'année dernière, je suis allé au Canada et c'était très génial. Après être arrivés, on est allés à l'hôtel où les chambres étaient exceptionnelles. On s'est bien amusés! Le meilleur jour était le premier samedi quand on a nagé avec des poissons extraordinaires et on a parlé pendant des heures avec les habitants de la région.
L'année prochaine, j'irai encore en France, mais je voyagerai avec

mes copains pour la première fois. J'ai l'intention de passer deux semaines à la plage!

43. Types of holiday
Writing
1 Sample answer:
Il y a six personnes.
Je vois la plage.
Ils sont contents.
Il y a une famille.

Listening
2 A D E

44. Where to stay
Reading
1 A E F

Speaking
2 Sample answers for follow-on questions:
(a) J'adore faire du camping avec mes amis.
(b) Je pense que les vacances au bord de la mer sont géniales.

45. Booking accommodation
Speaking
1 Sample answers:
1 Bonjour. Vous voulez rester combien de temps?
Je voudrais rester deux nuits.
Pas de problème.
2 Qui est dans votre groupe?
Il y a mon ami et moi.
Très bien.
3 Qu'est-ce que vous voulez voir dans la région?
Je voudrais visiter le musée.
Très bien.
4 Pourquoi aimez-vous faire du camping?
Ce n'est pas cher.
Je comprends.
5 Vous avez une question?
Il y a un bus pour aller au centre-ville?
Oui, il y a un bus toutes les vingt minutes, l'arrêt de bus est en face.

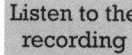

Listening
2 (a) 16th April (b) 3rd floor (c) a lift (d) a wheelchair
(e) 8.00 pm

46. Holiday activities
Writing
1 Sample answer:
Quand je suis en vacances, j'aime visiter les ponts célèbres ou aller aux musées car l'histoire m'intéresse beaucoup. Cependant, mon activité préférée en vacances est de manger des choses locales parce que je pense que c'est important d'avoir de nouvelles expériences.
Il y a un mois, j'ai passé mes vacances en Algérie avec ma famille et nous avons fait des sports extrêmes. C'était passionnant mais assez dangereux!
L'année prochaine, je vais voir un match de football en Angleterre car j'aimerais voir mon équipe de foot préférée.

Speaking
2 Sample answer:
Sur la photo, il y a cinq personnes qui jouent au basket dans un parc. Il fait beau et les jeunes gens portent des baskets. Je crois qu'ils s'amusent bien et c'est peut-être une équipe scolaire. À l'arrière-plan,

il y a des arbres et je vois que le ciel est bleu, alors c'est en été, à mon avis.
(a) Normalement, je visite des bâtiments intéressants.
(b) Récemment, j'ai essayé des plats traditionnels dans un restaurant en France.

47. Trips and excursions
Reading
1 (a) I love visiting / to visit historic towns.
(b) Nature interests me a lot.
(c) I want to travel abroad with my family.
(d) Last week I went to a beautiful village.
(e) My little brother likes the view of / from the bridge.

Listening
2 (a) A (b) B (c) A (d) C

48. Asking for help or directions
Speaking
1 Sample answers:
1 Bonjour. Je peux vous aider?
La piscine n'est pas propre.
2 Je suis désolé(e). Vous vous appelez comment?
Je m'appelle Mark.
3 D'accord. Vous restez combien de nuits?
Je reste trois nuits.
4 Merci. Que pensez-vous du camping?
Il est très bien.
5 D'accord. Vous avez une question?
Où est la ville?
La ville est dix minutes à pied d'ici. Sortez du camping et prenez la première rue à gauche.

Listening
2 (a) A (b) B (c) A

49. Shopping for gifts
Speaking
1 Sample answers:
1 Bonjour. Je peux vous aider?
Je voudrais acheter un livre.
2 C'est pour qui?
C'est pour mon ami.
3 Pourquoi est-ce que vous achetez ce cadeau?
C'est pour son anniversaire.
4 Voilà! Ça va?
J'aime ce livre.
5 D'accord. Vous avez une question?
C'est combien?
Ce livre coûte sept euros.

Listening
2 B D

50. Tourist information
Reading
1 (a) B (b) A (c) B (d) C

Speaking
2 Read aloud text

51. Tourist attractions
Writing
1 Sample answers:
Il y a un grand bâtiment.
Je vois un parc.
Il y a deux touristes.
Les touristes regardent le bâtiment.

Listening
2 (a) B (b) C (c) A

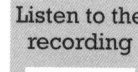

52. Holiday problems
Reading
1   B D F

Listening
2   (a) by plane
    (b) 12.00 / midnight
    (c) Toni left her money in her bedroom; her aunt lost her jacket
    (d) they were sick / ill and her aunt saw / went to see the doctor

53. Accommodation problems
Reading
1   A B F

Writing
2   Sample answer:
J'aime aller en vacances, mais il y a souvent des problèmes avec le logement. En juillet, j'ai passé une semaine dans un mauvais hôtel avec mon oncle préféré. Ma chambre n'était pas propre et il y avait trop de bruit dans le restaurant le soir. Aussi, il n'y avait pas d'ascenseur. L'année prochaine, je voudrais faire du camping.

54. Eating out
Writing
1   Sample answer:
Dans ma ville, mon restaurant préféré sert de la cuisine française. J'adore ce restaurant car les pâtes et le poisson sont délicieux et il est très agréable. Je vais aller à ce restaurant demain pour l'anniversaire de mon père et je vais bien m'amuser!

Speaking
2   Sample answers:
    1   Bonjour. Qu'est-ce que vous voulez manger?
       Je voudrais manger du poisson avec du riz.
    2   D'accord. C'est tout?
       C'est combien, les légumes?
       Le prix des légumes est quatre euros.
    3   Quelle est votre boisson préférée?
       Je préfère le café.
    4   Qu'est-ce que vous allez manger demain?
       Je vais manger un gâteau au chocolat.
    5   Vous avez une question?
       Le restaurant ouvre à quelle heure?
       Nous ouvrons à onze heures.

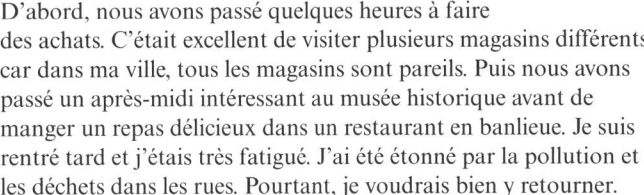

55. Opinions about food
Reading
1   C E F

Listening
2   1   Mon père **aime** les **légumes**.
    2   Je ne **mange** pas de **poulet**.
    3   Ma **mère** adore les **fraises**.
    4   Je veux prendre une glace.
    5   Les pâtes sont excellentes.
    6   Mes amis détestent le poisson.

56. The weather
Writing
1   (a) J'aime quand il fait chaud.
    (b) Je vais à la plage le week-end.
    (c) Quand il fait mauvais, je reste à la maison / chez moi.
    (d) La semaine dernière, il a neigé tous les jours.
    (e) S'il fait froid, je suis triste.

Listening
2   (a) B   (b) A   (c) A

57. Customs and festivals
Speaking
Sample answers:
1   Bonjour. Je peux vous aider?
    Je voudrais visiter un événement culturel.
    Ah oui!
2   Vous restez pour combien de temps ici?
    Je passe trois nuits ici.
    Très bien.
3   Qu'est-ce que vous allez faire demain?
    Je vais aller au cinéma.
    Intéressant.
4   Vous avez une question?
    Il y a des festivals dans la région?
    Oui, il y a deux festivals en juillet.
5   Vous avez une autre question?
    Pouvez-vous me recommander un hôtel?
    Bien sûr. L'hôtel Atlantique est un bon hôtel.

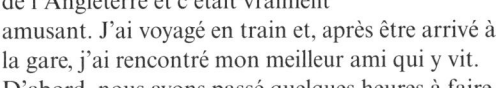

Writing
2   Sample answers:
    (a) J'adore les festivals.
    (b) J'aime les événements culturels dans ma ville.
    (c) Mon ami français trouve les concerts intéressants.
    (d) La semaine dernière, je suis allé(e) à une fête avec mes copains.
    (e) Je veux visiter Paris le 14 juillet.

58. Visiting a city
Speaking
1   Sample answer:
Il y a deux jours, je suis allé dans une grande ville qui se trouve dans le sud de l'Angleterre et c'était vraiment amusant. J'ai voyagé en train et, après être arrivé à la gare, j'ai rencontré mon meilleur ami qui y vit. D'abord, nous avons passé quelques heures à faire des achats. C'était excellent de visiter plusieurs magasins différents car dans ma ville, tous les magasins sont pareils. Puis nous avons passé un après-midi intéressant au musée historique avant de manger un repas délicieux dans un restaurant en banlieue. Je suis rentré tard et j'étais très fatigué. J'ai été étonné par la pollution et les déchets dans les rues. Pourtant, je voudrais bien y retourner.

Speaking
2   Sample answer:
Sur la photo, il y a des adolescents qui visitent une grande ville. Il y a un grand bâtiment au fond et aussi un feu rouge. Il pleut et les personnes marchent dans la rue. Ils portent tous une veste. Il y a un magasin à gauche où on peut acheter des cadeaux et des souvenirs.

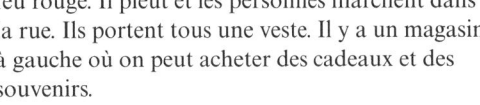

(a) J'adore visiter les grandes villes. C'est intéressant.
(b) Récemment, je suis allé(e) au supermarché où j'ai acheté du fromage.

59. School subjects
Listening
1   (a) art, science
    (b) media

Reading
2   (a) Maxime   (b) Enzo   (c) Enzo   (d) Maxime   (e) Eva   (f) Eva

60. School likes, dislikes and reasons
Reading
1 (a) it's quite hard (b) he's interested in reading (c) refused to explain something (d) a test in technology (e) he wants good marks

Speaking
2 Sample answers for follow-on questions:
(a) Je préfère les maths.
(b) Je déteste les devoirs.

61. Timetable and school day
Writing
1 (a) J'aime aller à l'école / au collège.
(b) Ma matière préférée est l'anglais.
(c) Mon frère déteste les maths car il trouve ça très difficile.
(d) L'année dernière j'ai eu beaucoup de devoirs.
(e) Si j'ai de bonnes notes, je peux continuer mon éducation.

Listening
2 (a) A (b) B (c) B (d) C

62. Equipment and facilities in school
Writing
1 Sample answer :
Mon collège est assez petit et il y a seulement 500 élèves. Il y a un gymnase mais il n'y a pas de piscine. J'aime mon collège car les profs sont sympas et on a beaucoup de tablettes et d'ordinateurs portables qu'on peut utiliser en classe.
La semaine dernière, je suis allé à l'école à pied car j'étais trop en retard pour le bus! À l'avenir, je voudrais rester à mon école et je vais étudier les maths et les sciences.

Listening
2 (a) useful (b) library (c) field

63. School uniform
Reading
1 (a) not fashionable (b) hides differences between rich and poor; can encourage good behaviour (c) colours must change (of uniform) (d) more comfortable clothes

Listening
2 B C E

64. Class activities
Reading
1 A C D

Listening
2 (a) his headteacher
(b) He would like to go on the exchange, but his parents won't allow him to.
(c) discover a different culture and make new friends
(d) that his parents will change their minds

65. School rules
Speaking
1 Sample answer:
(a) Selon moi, les règles de mon école sont assez justes. Par exemple, il faut écouter les profs pendant les cours et respecter les autres élèves. Cependant, on ne peut pas utiliser son portable au collège et je ne suis pas d'accord. Hier, mon ami a essayé de téléphoner à sa mère qui était malade, mais le prof a pris son portable.
(b) Si j'étais directeur, je changerais les règles scolaires parce qu'elles sont trop strictes, à mon avis. Les élèves ne porteraient pas d'uniforme et les cours commenceraient à dix heures car je déteste me lever tôt le matin!

(c) Je suis contre l'uniforme car ce n'est pas confortable et je n'aime pas porter de cravate. Mon meilleur ami aime notre uniforme car il dit que c'est pratique. Mais moi, je ne suis pas d'accord!

Listening
2 (a) There are too many rules.
(b) He was listening to music on his phone. / He was seen by a teacher.
(c) comfortable / practical
(d) He doesn't mind it. / He's neither for nor against it.

66. Opinions about school
Writing
1 Sample answer:
J'aime mon collège car les profs essaient toujours de m'aider avec mon travail scolaire et je les trouve vraiment sympas. Hier, mon prof de maths m'a expliqué un problème que j'avais avec un aspect difficile de la matière et j'étais très stressé. Ce qui me plaît au collège, ce sont les bâtiments modernes et aussi le directeur qui est travailleur. Par contre, je n'aime pas les règles puisqu'elles sont trop sévères.
La semaine dernière, j'ai participé à un spectacle de musique et c'était excellent. Je joue d'un instrument depuis six ans et j'étais très heureux de pouvoir jouer dans un groupe.
L'année prochaine, j'irai au lycée où j'étudierai les langues parce que je voudrais devenir prof dans le futur. Je pense qu'apprendre une langue est important et utile si on veut trouver un emploi bien payé.

Listening
2 B C F

67. Clubs and activities
Writing
1 J'aime aller aux clubs au collège. Mon activité préférée est l'athlétisme. Je cours souvent avec mes amis le jeudi après avoir fini les cours. Le mois dernier, on a participé à un concours sportif et j'ai gagné. À l'avenir je voudrais vraiment essayer d'apprendre un instrument de musique car c'est amusant.

Reading
2 (a) I like school clubs.
(b) My friends have a cookery lesson on Mondays.
(c) I hate drama because it's difficult.
(d) Last week, I played football after the last lesson.
(e) I'm going to rest.

68. Success at school
Speaking
1 Sample answer:
Je crois que j'ai toujours bien travaillé et j'ai fait mes devoirs tous les jours, alors je pense que je vais réussir tous mes examens. Mes profs me disent que je suis fort(e) en maths et en science, mais je voudrais aussi avoir de bonnes notes en français car je trouve cette matière très utile.

Reading
2 (a) B (b) B (c) C

69. Options at 16
Speaking
1 Sample answer:
J'ai déjà décidé de continuer mes études en histoire et en anglais car je suis fort en langues, mais je ne sais pas quelle autre matière choisir. Je suis faible en maths et en sciences et je n'aime pas l'art, alors je vais demander des conseils à mes profs avant de me décider.

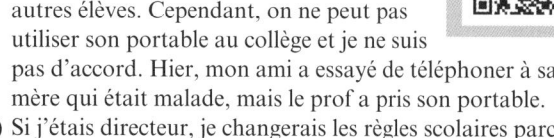

Reading

2 (a) B (b) A (c) C (d) A (e) A

Listening

3 (a) History (b) French (c) Music

70. Schools – France and the UK

Speaking

1 Sample answer:
Je préfère les écoles en France parce que les vacances d'été sont plus longues et il ne faut pas porter d'uniforme. L'année dernière, je suis allé à un collège français avec mon ami et c'était excellent. J'ai trouvé les professeurs plus sympas et les repas étaient vraiment délicieux.

Reading

2 B C F

71. Future study plans

Speaking

1 Sample answer:
Il y a beaucoup d'étudiants à l'université. Au premier plan, il y a trois étudiants. Une jeune femme regarde peut-être son emploi du temps, le jeune homme est en train de regarder sa tablette et la deuxième jeune femme au premier plan regarde son portable. Ils portent un sac. Il y a une étudiante qui est en fauteuil roulant. Le jeune homme au centre porte une veste et il a les cheveux courts et noirs.
(a) Je pense qu'aller à l'université est important pour mon futur.
(b) Je voudrais aller à l'université pour étudier l'anglais.

Reading

2 (a) Mathis

His future education plans	study at a university in England
Reason why	improve his English

(b) Sacha

Her future education plans	apprenticeship
Reason why	university is too expensive / she will be paid

72. Future plans

Reading

1 (a) B (b) C (c) A (d) A

Listening

2 (a) doctor
   (b) long training / expensive university
   (c) forget daily worries
   (d) doesn't know if she will marry

73. Part-time jobs and money

Writing

1 Sample answers:
Je vois quatre personnes.
Il y a une table.
La fille travaille dans un café.
Elle a les cheveux blonds.

Reading

2 A D E

74. Opinions about jobs

Writing

1 Sample answer:
Je pense que travailler est important car on peut gagner de l'argent mais on doit aussi être heureux quand on travaille. Je ne veux pas travailler dans un bureau parce que ce n'est pas intéressant. Le mois dernier, j'ai trouvé un poste dans un magasin qui se trouve près de ma maison. C'est facile et bien payé, alors j'ai pu acheter des livres et des vêtements avec l'argent que j'ai gagné.
Dans le futur, mon travail idéal serait dans un collège ou un lycée, car je voudrais être professeur de technologie.

Listening

2 Part 1: (a) B (b) B (c) A
  Part 2: (a) B (b) C (c) A

75. Job adverts and skills needed

Speaking

1 Sample answers for follow-on questions:
   (a) J'aime travailler dans un café.
   (b) Ma patronne est travailleuse et responsable.

Reading

2 (a) checkout / till
   (b) good at maths / like talking to customers

76. Applying for jobs

Speaking

1 Sample answers:
   1 Bonjour. Qu'est-ce que vous voulez?
      Je cherche un emploi.
      Très bien.
   2 Vous avez une question?
      Quel est le salaire?
      Le salaire est vingt euros de l'heure.
   3 Pourquoi voulez-vous travailler en France?
      Je veux améliorer mon français.
      Très bien.
   4 Qu'est-ce que vous allez faire après le travail le soir?
      Je vais aller au cinéma.
      Intéressant.
   5 Vous avez une autre question?
      Est-ce que les heures sont longues?
      Neuf heures du matin jusqu'à trois heures de l'après-midi.

Writing

2 Sample answers:
Il y a deux personnes.
Elles sont dans un bureau.
Je vois un ordinateur.
Il y a une table.

77. Volunteering

Speaking

1 Sample answer:
Je vois un jeune homme qui doit avoir faim parce qu'on lui donne de la nourriture. Il porte un chapeau et il a les cheveux châtains. Il y a des légumes et de la viande sur une assiette et le jeune homme va en manger. Il y a une femme à côté de lui et elle attend aussi une assiette de nourriture. Deux personnes servent et je pense qu'ils aident les jeunes. Je peux aussi voir des fruits.
(a) Chaque samedi, je travaille dans un café où on donne des boissons gratuites aux pauvres.
(b) La semaine dernière, j'ai travaillé pour une association qui aide les gens qui dorment dans la rue.

Listening

2 (a) B (b) C (c) B

78. Equality and helping others

Reading

1 (a) A (b) B (c) A

149

Writing
2 (a) L'égalité est importante.
   (b) J'aime aider les gens.
   (c) Mes parents donnent de l'argent à une association locale.
   (d) L'année dernière, j'ai commencé à travailler avec des jeunes en ville.
   (e) Je veux voir une société juste où tout le monde est égal.

79. The natural world
Writing
1 Sample answers:
Il y a cinq personnes.
Ils marchent.
Ils sont à la campagne.
Il fait beau.
Reading
2 C E F

80. Spending time in the countryside
Speaking
1 Sample answers for follow-on questions:
   (a) J'aime regarder les animaux.
   (b) J'aime la nature.
Listening
2 (a) B (b) A (c) C

81. The environment and me
Listening
1 (a) need to protect trees
   (b) demonstrated / protested against pollution
   (c) no problems with the environment
Writing
2 Je veux aider l'environnement car je pense que c'est très important. Je recycle toujours le papier et le verre. La semaine dernière, mes amis / copains ont réutilisé des sacs en plastique au supermarché. On devrait réduire la circulation dans les villes. Moi, je vais arrêter de voyager en voiture à l'avenir / dans le futur. Il ne faut pas ignorer la pollution!

82. Local environmental issues
Listening
1 (a) bus
   (b) by car
   (c) an electric car
   (d) clean
Reading
2 A C E

83. Global environmental issues
Listening
1 1 Il y a des **catastrophes mondiales** comme des **incendies**.
   2 On doit recycler le **verre**, le **métal** et le **carton**.
   3 Je prends le bus ou le train.
   4 Il faut réduire les déchets.
   5 Je veux aider les animaux en danger.
   6 Je déteste la pollution industrielle.
Reading
2 (a) environmental disasters / catastrophes (that have happened in different countries)
   (b) floods, more than 50,000 animals died
   (c) endangered species
   (d) throw away rubbish
   (e) they will eat plastic and become ill

84. Caring for the planet
Speaking
1 Sample answers:
   (a) Selon moi, nous devons parler au gouvernement qui pourrait commencer à réduire la pollution et arrêter le changement climatique. Si tout le monde fait quelque chose, nous réussirons, mais si on ne fait rien, la planète est en danger.
   (b) Récemment, ma famille et moi avons commencé à recycler plus. Nous recyclons le papier et le plastique depuis quelques années, mais le mois dernier, ma mère m'a dit qu'il faut recycler aussi les vêtements qu'on ne porte plus. Donc mon frère et moi, nous avons pris nos vieux vêtements et nous les avons donnés aux magasins qui les vendent aux gens qui n'ont pas beaucoup d'argent. Nos vêtements aident les pauvres, et ils ne sont plus jetés comme les déchets. C'est mieux pour la planète!
   (c) Pour sauver notre planète, je vais prendre le bus pour aller au collège. Je pense que si nous réduisons le nombre de voitures dans nos rues, nous allons réduire la pollution en ville. Cela vaut la peine à mon avis, parce que c'est meilleur pour la santé, et en plus, tout le monde serait moins stressé avec moins de circulation!
Reading
2 (a) I like my family and my friends a lot.
   (b) The planet is very important to me.
   (c) We must help organisations / charities / associations to save the Earth.
   (d) Yesterday I recycled some plastic (things).
   (e) In the future, I'm going to protect endangered animals.

85. A greener future
Writing
1 Sample answer:
Dans ma région, il y a beaucoup de trains et de bus, mais les gens utilisent trop les voitures. Je pense que c'est nul car il y a beaucoup de pollution en ville. À mon avis, les transports en commun sont excellents parce que les bus sont toujours propres et les trains ne sont pas en retard.
La semaine dernière, j'ai refusé des sacs en plastique au supermarché et j'ai réutilisé des sacs en papier. À l'avenir, je vais acheter un nouveau vélo car je ne voudrais pas utiliser une voiture qui cause de la pollution.
Reading
2 (a) extinction of species; not enough green spaces
   (b) build too much
   (c) serious

86. Practice for Paper 1: Speaking
1 Sample answer:
   1 Bonjour. Vous voulez rester combien de temps?
      Je voudrais rester deux nuits.
      Pas de problème.
   2 Il y a combien de personnes dans votre groupe?
      Il y a trois personnes.
      Très bien.
   3 Qu'est-ce que vous voulez comme repas ici?
      Je voudrais le petit-déjeuner.
      Très bien.
   4 Pourquoi êtes-vous en France?
      Je visite la région.
      Je comprends.
   5 Vous avez une question?
      Il y a un restaurant à l'hôtel?
      Oui, le voilà.

2 Sample answers for follow-up questions:
(a) J'aime faire du vélo.
(b) Je m'entends bien avec ma famille.

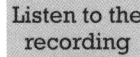

3 Sample answer:
Sur la photo je peux voir une salle de classe avec sept élèves et un prof. Il a les cheveux courts et il porte une chemise blanche. Il parle aux jeunes. Les élèves portent un uniforme scolaire. Ils écoutent le prof et ils sont contents.
(a) Ma matière préférée, c'est les maths.
(b) J'aime mon uniforme car il est confortable.

Extended conversation sample answers:
(a) Il y a beaucoup de clubs scolaires. Moi, je vais au club de foot après les cours le mercredi parce que je suis très sportif et j'aime jouer avec mes amis.
(b) Hier, au collège, j'ai eu cours de français et c'était génial. J'ai parlé avec mes amis et j'ai mangé des pâtes. J'ai trouvé le repas délicieux. L'après-midi, j'ai eu deux cours de sport où on a joué au foot.
(c) À l'avenir, je vais aller à l'université, car je voudrais être professeur de sport. C'est parfait pour moi parce que j'aime aider les jeunes et je suis vraiment sportif.

87. Practice for Paper 1: Speaking

1 Sample answers:
1 Bonjour. Vous êtes en visite ici?
Je voudrais visiter le château.
2 Ah oui? Vous aimez le centre-ville?
Oui, c'est génial.
3 Vous avez une question?
Pour aller aux magasins?
Prenez la première rue à gauche.
4 Vous voulez faire quoi là?
Je veux acheter un cadeau.
5 Parfait ! Vous avez une autre question?
Il y a un bus pour aller au château?
Oui, toutes les vingt minutes.

2 Sample answers for follow-on questions:
(a) J'aime manger des pâtes.
(b) Je pense qu'il ne faut pas manger de viande.

3 Sample answer:
Sur la photo, je peux voir une famille à table dans un jardin. Je crois qu'il fait beau. Il y a six personnes qui vont manger un repas préparé par le père. Sur la table, il y a des légumes et des verres d'eau et tout le monde est en train de sourire parce qu'ils sont très contents.
(a) J'aime jouer au foot.
(b) Le week-end dernier, je suis allé(e) au bord de la mer avec ma famille.

Extended conversation sample answers:
(a) Dans ma famille, il y a cinq personnes: mes parents, mon frère qui a douze ans et qui s'appelle Lucas, ma sœur qui est très grande, et moi. Je m'entends bien avec ma mère car elle me respecte, mais de temps en temps, je trouve mon père un peu difficile puisqu'il est trop sévère.
(b) La semaine dernière, je suis allé en ville avec mes copains. Après y être arrivés en bus, nous avons fait les magasins et j'ai réussi à acheter un petit cadeau pour ma meilleure copine qui aura bientôt seize ans. Avant de rentrer, nous avons pris un repas délicieux dans un petit café près de la gare.
(c) À l'avenir, je voudrais travailler pour une association qui aide les pauvres ou les animaux. Je pense qu'il est vraiment important d'aider les autres et je vais essayer d'améliorer la vie des autres.

88. Practice for Paper 2: Listening

1 B C E
2 (a) A (b) A (c) B (d) C (e) C
3 (a) at the seaside (b) in the south-east of France
4 Jade likes: camping; dislikes: renting an apartment / flat
Pierre likes: a swimming pool; dislikes: no restaurant

89. Practice for Paper 2: Listening

1 B D E
2 (a) A (b) B (c) A (d) B (e) A (f) C
3 1 Le **meilleur sport** est l'**équitation**.
   2 J'aime **aussi** le **hockey** et la **plongée**.
   3 Il faut être souvent actif.
   4 Mon régime est tellement sain!
   5 J'évite la viande et le poisson.
   6 On doit boire moins de boissons sucrées.

90. Practice for Paper 3: Reading

1 (a) Enzo (b) Alex (c) Alex (d) Clara (e) Enzo (f) Clara
2 (a) rainy (b) a castle (c) the stadium

91. Practice for Paper 3: Reading

1 (a) B (b) C (c) A (d) B (e) A
2 (a) C (b) A (c) research in a museum (d) free / at liberty

92. Practice for Paper 4: Writing

1 Sample answers:
Il y a six personnes.
Un garçon a un portable.
Les filles ont les cheveux noirs.
Il y a deux sacs.
2 Sample answer:
Le centre commercial est dans ma ville. Il y a beaucoup de magasins qui sont excellents. Mon magasin préféré est un magasin de vêtements car j'aime la mode. Je vais aller au centre demain avec ma mère car je vais acheter une nouvelle jupe.
3 Sample answer:
Dans ma famille, il y a quatre personnes. J'ai un frère qui s'appelle Thomas et il a dix-huit ans. Je m'entends bien avec lui parce qu'il est génial. Mon père travaille dans un bureau et ma mère, qui est professeur, est très sympa.
Mon meilleur ami, Lucas, est vraiment sympa et il aime les mêmes sports que moi, alors on s'entend très bien.
La semaine dernière, je suis allé à la piscine avec mes amis et nous avons fait de la natation ensemble. C'était excellent.
La semaine prochaine, je vais sortir au restaurant au centre-ville avec ma famille pour l'anniversaire de mon frère.

4   (a) J'aime ma ville.
    (b) Ma maison est très grande.
    (c) Je joue au foot dans le jardin.
    (d) La semaine dernière, je suis allé(e) aux magasins avec mon frère.
    (e) Je peux faire du vélo samedi à la campagne.

93. Practice for Paper 4: Writing

1 Sample answer:
À mon avis, les vacances sont importantes puisqu'il faut se reposer après avoir beaucoup travaillé pendant l'année. On peut aussi se faire de nouveaux amis. Je pense qu'aller à l'étranger est amusant parce qu'on peut apprendre beaucoup de choses sur la culture d'un autre pays et même apprendre une autre langue. L'année dernière, je suis allé à Paris avec ma famille et nous nous sommes très bien amusés. On a logé dans un hôtel excellent et il faisait chaud, alors j'ai pu faire de la natation dans la piscine. En été, nous irons au Canada et j'ai l'intention de parler français avec les gens.

2 Sample answer:
J'ai un portable que j'adore et je crois que je ne pourrais pas vivre sans la technologie ! J'ai aussi une tablette que j'utilise tous les jours. Internet est important car on peut envoyer des messages et des e-mails tous les jours, ce qui permet de rester en contact avec les copains et la famille. Cependant, il y a aussi des problèmes comme le harcèlement en ligne et il y a aussi des risques comme le vol d'identité. Mon père pense qu'Internet est très dangereux. La semaine dernière, j'ai regardé un film en ligne avant de télécharger des chansons que j'ai écoutées samedi soir dans ma chambre. J'ai aussi décidé de parler avec mon copain qui habite en Martinique.
Ce week-end, je vais faire des jeux sur Internet car j'aime bien m'amuser avec mes amis. Je mettrai des photos de mes dernières vacances sur mon réseau social préféré et je regarderai un film avec mon frère.

3 J'aime aller à l'école. Ma matière préférée est l'anglais. Je fais toujours mes devoirs dans ma chambre avant de manger. La semaine dernière, mes amis et moi sommes allés au musée en ville. Je vais étudier à l'université à l'avenir car je veux trouver un très bon emploi.

Grammar exercises

94. Articles 1

A 1 les magasins
    2 la pharmacie
    3 les toilettes
    4 l'hôtel
    5 les cinémas
    6 le musée
    7 la gare
    8 le parking
    9 les rues
    10 l'appartement
B 1 un 2 une 3 une 4 un 5 une 6 une 7 un 8 un
C *le chien* – les chiens; un château – *des châteaux*; l'animal – *les animaux*; *une voiture* – des voitures; le nez – *les nez*; le bateau – *les bateaux*; un hôtel – *des hôtels*; l'arbre – les arbres; une page – des pages*; l'eau* – les eaux; une piscine – *des piscines*; *la ville* – les villes

95. Articles 2

A 1 du 2 de l' 3 des 4 du 5 des 6 du 7 des 8 de la 9 du 10 des
B 1 Je n'ai pas d'œufs. I have no eggs. 2 Je n'ai pas de thé. I have no tea. 3 Je n'ai pas d'eau. I haven't any water. 4 Je n'ai pas de viande. I haven't any meat. 5 Je n'ai pas de sucre. I have no sugar.
C 1 à la 2 au 3 aux 4 à la 5 à la 6 au 7 à l' 8 aux 9 à l' 10 au

96. Adjectives

A 1 Ma mère est petite.   2 Mon père est grand.
    3 Ma maison est belle.   4 Mon chat est noir.
    5 Elle est heureuse.   6 Les fenêtres sont chères.
B 1 gros 2 blancs 3 travailleuse 4 sportifs 5 tristes 6 agréable

C

grand	grande	**grands**	grandes	big / tall
petit	petite	**petits**	petites	small
noir	**noire**	noirs	**noires**	black
neuf	neuve	**neufs**	neuves	new
dernier	**dernière**	derniers	**dernières**	last
marron	**marron**	marron	**marron**	(chestnut) brown
triste	**triste**	tristes	**tristes**	sad
sérieux	**sérieuse**	sérieux	**sérieuses**	serious
actif	active	actifs	**actives**	active
amusant	**amusante**	amusants	**amusantes**	funny
vieux	vieille	**vieux**	vieilles	old
beau	belle	**beaux**	**belles**	beautiful
ancien	**ancienne**	anciens	**anciennes**	ancient
blanc	**blanche**	blancs	**blanches**	white
sportif	sportive	**sportifs**	sportives	**sporty**

D 1 Elle a de beaux yeux bleus
    2 Les meilleures fleurs jaunes
    3 Mes vieilles baskets blanches
    4 Mes pauvres parents malades

97. Possessives

A 1 Dans ma famille, il y a **mon** père, **ma** mère, **ma** sœur et **mes** deux frères. **Ma** grand-mère vient souvent chez nous avec **mon** grand-père. **Mon** amie adore **mes** grands-parents.
    2 Dans **sa** chambre, elle a **son** lit, **ses** livres, **son** bureau, **sa** télévision, **ses** vêtements, **son** portable et **son** sac.
    3 Dans **notre** collège, nous avons **nos** professeurs, **notre** bibliothèque, **notre** cour et **notre** terrain de sport. Et vous, qu'est-ce que vous avez dans **votre** collège et dans **vos** salles de classe? Vous avez **vos** tableaux blancs et **votre** gymnase?
    4 (a) Comment s'appellent ton père et ta mère?
       (b) Qu'est-ce que tu achètes avec ton argent?
       (c) C'est quand ton anniversaire?
       (d) Qu'est-ce qu'il y a dans ta ville ou ton village?
    5 Dans leur ville, ils ont leur hôtel, leurs cinémas, leur pharmacie, leur boulangerie, leurs cafés, leurs parcs, leur hôpital, leur école et tous leurs petits magasins.

B Sample answers:
Mon fromage est très moderne; Nos amies ne sont pas très tristes; Leurs photos sont assez jaunes; Vos gâteaux sont très justes.

98. Comparisons

A Lucie est la plus grande. Tom est le moins grand.
B *Other examples:* Anna est pire qu'Antoine en français. Anna est la meilleure en Technologie.
C 1 Philippe est aussi grand que Sara. = Philippe is as tall as Sara.
    2 Les maths sont plus difficiles que la musique. = Maths is more difficult than music.
    3 Les frites sont moins saines que les fruits. = Chips are not as healthy as fruit.
    4 Une cravate est moins confortable qu'un jogging. = A tie is less comfortable than trousers.
    5 La science est aussi intéressante que l'anglais. = Science is as interesting as English.

99. Other adjectives and pronouns
A 1 cette 2 ce 3 cette 4 ces 5 ce 6 cette 7 ces 8 cet 9 cette 10 cet
B 1 Quelle 2 Quelle 3 Quel 4 quel 5 Quelles 6 Quels 7 Quel 8 quels
C 1 quelque 2 quelques 3 autre 4 autre 5 quelque 6 autres 7 quelques 8 autres

100. Adverbs
A 1 malheureusement 2 extrêmement 3 probablement 4 vraiment 5 certainement 6 complètement
B Le matin, <u>d'abord</u>, je me lève à sept heures, <u>puis d'habitude</u>, je prends mon petit-déjeuner. <u>Ensuite</u>, je quitte la maison. <u>Finalement</u>, j'arrive au collège à huit heures et demie, mais c'est <u>souvent</u> trop tôt. <u>Alors</u>, <u>à l'avenir</u>, je vais rester au lit plus longtemps.
In the morning, first I get up at 7 o'clock then usually I have my breakfast. Then I leave the house. Finally, I arrive at school at half past eight, but it is often too early. So, in the future, I am going to stay in bed longer.
C Souvent mes grands-parents viennent avec nous, et c'est vraiment pratique car ils font régulièrement du baby-sitting. Cependant, de temps en temps, ils se sentent vraiment fatigués et ils ne sont pas toujours à l'aise, donc ils ne viendront pas l'année prochaine. À l'avenir, ils viendront seulement s'ils sont absolument en forme!
D Sample answers:
J'aime <u>toujours</u> les fêtes.
Nous jouons <u>souvent</u> de la musique <u>ensemble</u>.
L'examen était <u>vraiment</u> difficile.
Elle joue <u>régulièrement</u> au tennis dans un club.

101. Object pronouns
A 1 We see you. 2 Do you know him? 3 I want to see her. 4 You meet us. 5 She will forget you. 6 I will lose them.
B 1 I am passing my books to you.
2 Don't speak / talk to him.
3 We will give him / her a mobile phone.
4 He is going to send us a present.
5 You will tell them the story.
C 1 Vous comprenez le professeur? Nous le comprenons souvent.
2 Elle aime les sports d'hiver? Elle ne les aime pas du tout.
3 Tu vas vendre ton vélo? Oui, je vais le vendre demain.
4 Il veut acheter la maison? Non, il ne veut pas l'acheter.
D 1 Il les cherche.
2 Nous lui envoyons un cadeau.
3 Il leur a donné des livres.
4 Tu leur as téléphoné?

102. More pronouns: *y* and *en*
A 1 Il va y habiter.
2 Elle y a vu ses amis.
3 Vous y jouez?
4 J'y suis arrivé avant les autres.
5 Tu y es allée ce matin?
B 1 J'en fais beaucoup.
2 Elle n'en fait pas.
3 Non, j'en ai trois.
4 Ils en mangent tous les samedis.
5 Il y en a plusieurs.
C 1 J'y vais de temps en temps.
2 … et j'en mange beaucoup.
3 … je n'en mange jamais …
4 … j'y suis allé …
5 … tu veux y aller …?
6 … mon frère n'en mange pas …

103. Other pronouns
A 1 Le repas que j'ai pris était excellent.
2 C'est Claude qui est le plus beau.
3 Ce sont mes parents qui adorent la viande.
4 Voilà le chapeau qu'il a perdu.
5 Où sont les robes qui sont bleues?
6 La tour que j'ai visitée était vieille.
7 L'homme qui monte dans le train est petit.
8 Ma copine qui s'appelle Mathilde a seize ans.
9 Quel est le film que tu veux voir?
B 1 Le repas que nous avons mangé était excellent. = The meal which we ate was excellent.
2 les pâtes? J'en ai mangé beaucoup. = Pasta? I have eaten lots of it.
3 Le café où je vais le samedi est fermé. = The café where I go on Saturdays is closed.
4 Le cinéma Gaumont? J'y suis allée pour voir 'Les Minions'. = The Gaumont cinema? I went there to see 'Les Minions'.

104. Present tense: *-er* verbs
A aimer: j'aime, nous aimons, ils aiment
donner: je donne, nous donnons, ils donnent
habiter: j'habite, nous habitons, ils habitent
inviter: j'invite, nous invitons, ils invitent
jouer: je joue, nous jouons, ils jouent
marcher: je marche, nous marchons, ils marchent
parler: je parle, nous parlons, ils parlent
quitter: je quitte, nous quittons, ils quittent
regarder: je regarde, nous regardons, ils regardent
trouver: je trouve, nous trouvons, ils trouvent
B 1 vous parlez 2 elle invite 3 tu habites 4 nous trouvons 5 il regarde 6 vous marchez 7 tu donnes 8 elle quitte 9 il joue 10 ils / elles regardent
C *-ger* verbs:
1 ils bougent 2 nous téléchargeons 3 nous changeons 4 je mange
-yer verbs:
5 tu envoies 6 vous payez 7 j'essaie 8 nous envoyons
-ler / -ter verbs:
1 je m'appelle 2 ils jettent 3 nous nous rappelons 4 elle s'appelle
acheter-type verbs:
5 tu achètes 6 elles préfèrent 7 vous vous levez 8 il achète
D 1 Ils habitent en France? Do they live in France?
2 Marie mange de la viande? Does Marie eat meat?
3 Vous préférez la science? Do you prefer science?
4 Les sœurs jettent les fruits? Do the sisters throw out the fruit?
5 Mon copain et moi achetons des frites? Are my friend and I buying chips?

105. Present tense: *-ir* and *-re* verbs
A finir – to finish; prévenir – to warn; remplir – to fill; agir – to act; réussir – to succeed; obtenir – to obtain; choisir – to choose; réfléchir – to think about

B

	dormir	sortir
je	dors	sors
tu	dors	sors
il / elle	dort	sort
nous	dormons	sortons
vous	dormez	sortez
ils / elles	dorment	sortent

C 1 L'ami choisit un cadeau.
   2 Vous courez aux magasins.
   3 Nous finissons nos devoirs.
   4 Je remplis le verre de d'eau.

D

	vendre	prendre	écrire
je	vends	prends	écris
tu	vends	prends	écris
il / elle	vend	prend	écrit
nous	vendons	prenons	écrivons
vous	vendez	prenez	écrivez
ils / elles	vendent	prennent	écrivent

E 1 nous vendons   5 vous buvez
   2 ils répondent   6 elle lit
   3 je descends   7 je traduis
   4 tu prends   8 il comprend

106. *Avoir* and *être*

A 1 Elle a un chat.
   2 J'ai les cheveux blonds.
   3 Ils ont une grande maison.
   4 Il a onze ans.
   5 Nous avons un petit appartement.
   6 Vous avez un beau chien.
   7 Ma sœur a une jupe rouge.
   8 Les filles ont un problème.
   9 Tu as deux livres.
   10 Vous avez une nouvelle maison.
B 1 Ils / Elles ont un chien et trois chats.
   2 Tu as une sœur?
   3 Elle a les cheveux noirs.
   4 Nous avons une grande cuisine.
   5 J'ai trois enfants.
   6 J'ai seize ans.
   7 Il a une voiture.
C 1 Je suis français.
   2 Nous sommes tristes.
   3 Ma tante est assez petite.
   4 Vous êtes sportif mais calme.
   5 Mes yeux sont bleus.
   6 Tu es content?
   7 Les chiens sont grands.
   8 Je suis au chômage.
   9 Nous sommes canadiens.
   10 Il est agréable.
D Sample answers:
Les filles ont les cheveux marron.
Vos parents sont amusants.
Je suis grosse.
Nos chiens ont les yeux bleus et tristes.
L'homme a un grand chapeau rouge.
L'homme a une petite voiture noire.

107. Reflexive verbs

A 1 me 2 te 3 s' 4 s'
B 1 Je me suis coupé la main. 2 Elle s'est mariée.
   3 Nous nous sommes levé(e)s à huit heures.
   4 Il s'est demandé pourquoi. 5 Tu t'es beaucoup amusé(e).
C 1 F 2 A 3 D 4 B 5 H 6 C 7 E 8 G

108. Other important verbs

A

	devoir	pouvoir	vouloir	savoir
je	dois	peux	veux	sais
tu	dois	peux	veux	sais
il / elle / on	doit	peut	veut	sait
nous	devons	pouvons	voulons	savons
vous	devez	pouvez	voulez	savez
ils / elles	doivent	peuvent	veulent	savent

B 1 Pouvez-vous aider mon père?
   2 Sais-tu nager?
   3 Mes parents veulent acheter une nouvelle maison.
   4 On doit toujours s'arrêter au feu rouge.
   5 Voulez-vous danser avec moi ce soir?
   6 Elle sait déjà lire et écrire.
C 1 Elle veut trouver une chambre et nous aussi, *nous voulons trouver une chambre.*
   2 Les élèves peuvent louer un vélo et toi aussi, *tu peux louer un vélo.*
   3 Le pilote doit tout vérifier et vous aussi, *vous devez tout vérifier.*
   4 Elle sait faire la cuisine et eux aussi, *ils savent faire la cuisine.*
   5 Je peux faire du vélo et elles aussi, *elles peuvent faire du vélo.*
   6 Il ne peut jamais comprendre les règles et vous non plus, *vous ne pouvez jamais comprendre les règles.*
   7 Nous savons préparer les repas et moi aussi, *je sais préparer les repas.*
D *Examples:* On ne doit pas manger en classe. On ne veut pas répondre aux professeurs. On peut dormir en classe. On ne sait pas envoyer des textos.

109. The perfect tense 1

A Sample answers: J'ai vendu la maison. Elle a détesté le bateau. Nous avons fini les devoirs.
B 1 Elle a invité sa copine au match,
   2 Vous avez fini le repas?
   3 Ils ont travaillé au collège.
   4 Il a beaucoup neigé ce matin,
   5 Tu n'as pas mangé de légumes?
   6 Nous avons choisi un bon restaurant.
   7 Elle n'a pas oublié son livre.
   8 Ils ont attendu à l'aéroport.
   9 J'ai visité le musée.
   10 Nous n'avons pas entendu le bruit.
C 1 Nous n'avons pas perdu l'argent.
   2 Vous n'avez pas attendu les chiens.
   3 Je n'ai pas fini le pain.
   4 Elle n'a pas vendu le bateau.
   5 Il n'a pas détesté les devoirs.
D 1 J'ai mis le livre sur la table.
   2 Elle a écrit à son frère.
   3 Tu n'as rien fait au collège?
   4 Il n'a pas lu ma lettre.
   5 Nous avons pu acheter une voiture.
E 1 J'ai compris la situation.
   2 Il a vu un chien.
   3 Tu as pris un bus à la gare?
   4 Qu'est-ce que tu as fait?

110. The perfect tense 2

A 1 Elle est tombée.
   2 Mes copains sont arrivés trop tard.
   3 Les chats sont montés sur la table.
   4 Marie n'est pas descendue vite.
   5 Emma est allée à la piscine.
   6 Vous êtes retournés en France?
   7 Je ne suis pas parti tôt.
   8 Elles sont entrées dans la maison.
B 1 Élise est arrivée à 11 heures.
   2 Il est allé au collège.
   3 Nous sommes entrés, tous les garçons, dans le magasin.
   4 Marie n'est rentrée qu'à minuit.
   5 Mes stylos ne sont pas tombés.
   6 Il est sorti avec sa soeur.
C 1 elles sont montées très vite
   2 je suis arrivé(e)
   3 ils ne sont pas tombés
   4 elle est allée en ville

D
je me suis levé(e)
tu t'es levé(e)
il s'est levé
elle s'est levée
nous nous sommes levé(e)s
vous vous êtes levé(e)s
ils se sont levés
elles se sont levées
E 1 Elle s'est reposée sur la plage.   2 Ils se sont levés à
7 heures.   3 Je me suis bien entendu(e) avec mon frère.
4 Elle se sont intéressées à l'histoire.

111. The imperfect tense
A 1 *jouer*
   je jouais
   nous jouions
   ils jouaient
  2 *finir*
   je finissais
   nous finissions
   ils finissaient
  3 perdre
   je perdais
   nous perdions
   ils perdaient
  4 avoir
   j'avais
   nous avions
   ils avaient
  5 être
   j'étais
   nous étions
   ils étaient
  6 boire
   je buvais
   nous buvions
   ils buvaient
  7 aller
   j'allais
   nous allions
   ils allaient
  8 partir
   je partais
   nous partions
   ils partaient
  9 faire
   je faisais
   nous faisions
   ils faisaient
  10 lire
   je lisais
   nous lisions
   ils lisaient
  11 savoir
   je savais
   nous savions
   ils savaient
  12 prendre
   je prenais
   nous prenions
   ils prenaient

B 1 elle attendait   2 ils écrivaient
  3 il dormait   4 je regardais
  5 elles étaient contentes

C 1 Je jouais avec mon petit frère sur la plage. = I used to play with my little brother on the beach.
  2 Nous mangions très souvent ensemble. = We used to eat together very often.
  3 Il travaillait dans l'école. = He used to work in the school.
  4 On vendait beaucoup de glaces. = They used to sell lots of ice-cream.
  5 Ils faisaient du vélo. = They used to do / go cycling.
  6 Tu étais très content. = You used to be happy.

D J'allais au collège quand j'ai vu mon ami. Il y avait beaucoup de gens. J'ai dit «Bonjour».

112. The future tense
A 1 Il va sortir ce soir. = He is going to go out this evening.
  2 Nous allons vendre la maison. = We are going to sell the house.
  3 Vous allez bientôt comprendre. = You are going to understand soon.
  4 Tu vas partir en vacances. = You are going to go away on holiday.
  5 Ma mère va voir un concert. = My mother is going to see a concert.
  6 Les garçons vont arriver en retard. = The boys are going to arrive late.

B 1 Nous allons aller en ville demain.
  2 Quand vas-tu partir?
  3 Ils vont faire leurs devoirs.
  4 Vous allez jouer au tennis?
  5 Théo va faire la cuisine.
  6 Ses sœurs vont aider.

C 1 lavera   2 inviteras
  3 finirai   4 manquerez
  5 visitera   6 arriveront
  7 parleront   8 jouerai

D 1 ils devront   2 nous saurons
  3 je ferai   4 elle sera
  5 tu auras   6 elles viendront
  7 il verra   8 tu iras

E 1 they will have to   2 we will know
  3 I will do   4 she will be
  5 you will have   6 they will come
  7 he will see   8 you will go

113. The conditional tense
A

	vouloir	-er verbs	aller	avoir	être	faire
		jouer				
je	voudrais	jouerais	irais	aurais	serais	ferais
tu	voudrais	jouerais	irais	aurais	serais	ferais
il / elle	voudrait	jouerait	irait	aurait	serait	ferait

B 1 Ma mère habiterait une belle maison. = My mother would live in a beautiful house.
  2 Vous ne travailleriez plus. = You would no longer work.
  3 Nous visiterions beaucoup de pays. = We would visit lots of countries.
  4 Il donnerait de l'argent aux autres. = He would give money to others.
  5 Voudrais-tu mettre de l'argent à la banque? = Would you like to put some money in the bank?
  6 J'achèterais une nouvelle voiture. = I would buy a new car.

C 1 Je serais très riche.
  2 Est-ce que tu ferais de la natation?
  3 Il aurait beaucoup d'amis.
  4 Elle irait en France.

D Sample answers:
Si plus de gens utilisaient un vélo en ville, il y aurait moins de circulation.
Si on ne portait pas un uniforme, on serait plus confortable.
Si tu prends le métro, tu arriveras plus vite.
Si j'étudiais plus, j'aurais la possibilité d'aller à l'université.

114. Negatives
A ne … pas = not; ne … jamais = never; ne … rien = nothing, not anything; ne … personne = nobody, not anybody; ne … aucun = not any, none; ne … que = only; ne … ni … ni = neither … nor; ne … pas encore = not yet; ne … plus = no longer, no more

B 1 We like neither science nor history.
  2 I will no longer eat any meat.
  3 He never arrived.
  4 They found nothing.
  5 I am sending no emails.
  6 She only does two hours per month.
  7 He will never return / go back to France again.

C 1 Je n'ai aucun problème.
  2 Il ne va jamais au musée.
  3 Elles ne sont pas contentes.
  4 Il n'a rien bu.
  5 Je ne vais pas acheter de viande.

D 1 Nous ne mangerons plus de légumes.
  2 Elle n'a jamais dit bonjour.
  3 Tu ne rencontres que deux amies en ville.
  4 Il n'a rien compris.

115. The perfect infinitive and the present participle

A 1 avoir fait
2 avoir joué
3 avoir fini
4 avoir mis
5 avoir voulu
6 avoir écrit

B 1 F 2 A 3 E 4 B 5 D 6 C

C Après avoir choisi les légumes, elle a préparé un repas.
Après avoir mangé, il est allé au cinéma.
Après avoir discuté avec ses amis, il est rentré à la maison / chez lui.
Après avoir perdu ses clés, elle a pleuré.

D 1 Avant de faire ses devoirs, elle a téléchargé de la musique.
2 Avant de revenir, il a acheté une carte.
3 Avant de partir, il a dansé.
4 Avant de sortir, il a téléphoné à sa mère.

E 1 finissant 2 achetant 3 allant 4 disant
5 mangeant 6 faisant 7 prenant 8 ayant
9 partant 10 venant

F 1 écoutant 2 riant 3 travaillant
4 courant 5 regardant

116. The passive

A 1 E 2 A 3 F 4 B 5 C 6 D

B 1 The men were invited to a party.
2 I'm always helped by my teachers.
3 My flat has been sold.
4 The books were bought.
5 The story was written.

C 1 La maison sera vendue.
2 La porte a été ouverte.
3 Le fruit a été mangé.
4 Les chiens sont aimés.
5 Les boissons sont commandées.

117. Questions

A 1 Est-ce qu'il peut venir lundi?
2 Est-ce que vous avez une carte de la ville?
3 Est-ce que les élèves ont fini leurs devoirs?
4 Est-ce qu'elle veut aller en ville?
5 Est-ce que vous êtes professeur?
6 Est-ce que nous allons arriver au collège à huit heures?

B 1 C 2 D 3 E 4 B 5 A

C 1 B 2 H 3 D 4 E 5 A 6 G 7 F 8 C

D *Sample questions:* Où habites-tu? À quelle heure est-ce que tu te lèves le matin? Combien de frères est-ce que tu as? Qu'est-ce que tu aimes faire le week-end?

118. Speaking (Foundation)

1 Sample answers for follow-on questions:
(a) J'aime lire des livres.
(b) J'adore la musique.

SPEAKING TRACK 159 — Listen to the recording

2 Sample answers:
1 Bonjour. Je peux vous aider?
Je voudrais un cadeau.
2 C'est pour qui?
C'est pour mon père.
3 D'accord. C'est pour une fête spéciale?
C'est pour son anniversaire.
4 Voilà! Ça va?
C'est excellent.
5 D'accord. Vous avez une question?
C'est combien?
Dix euros.

SPEAKING TRACK 160 — Listen to the recording

3 Sample answer:

Picture 1
Il y a une professeur avec quatre élèves dans une salle de classe. Ils portent un uniforme scolaire, une chemise blanche et une cravate bleue, rouge et jaune. Les élèves écrivent. La professeur aide la fille avec son travail et elle est sympa. Elle a les cheveux châtains.

SPEAKING TRACK 161 — Listen to the recording

Picture 2
Il y a une jeune femme qui travaille dans un café. Elle porte de l'eau et du café et elle sert les gens. Il y a deux personnes à gauche qui mangent le déjeuner et à droite il y a une femme qui a les cheveux noirs. Je vois aussi des tables. La jeune femme a les cheveux blonds et elle est contente car elle sourit.
Sample answers to follow-on questions:

Picture 1
(a) Ma matière préférée est l'histoire car c'est vraiment intéressant.
(b) Je m'entends bien avec mes professeurs car ils sont sympas.

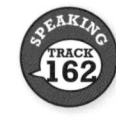

SPEAKING TRACK 162 — Listen to the recording

Picture 2
(a) Je préfère travailler dans un supermarché car c'est intéressant.
(b) Je veux être professeur car j'aime les enfants.

Studying and my future
Example of a grade 1 answer: J'aime mon école.
Example of a grade 2 answer: J'aime mon école. C'est intéressant et génial.
Example of a grade 5 answer: Je pense que mon école est excellente parce que les règles sont justes et les professeurs m'aident beaucoup et ils sont sympas. Selon moi, les bâtiments sont modernes et propres et je m'entends bien avec tout le monde. Je vais rester à mon école l'année prochaine car j'ai toujours été heureux ici.

SPEAKING TRACK 163 — Listen to the recording

119. Listening (Foundation)

1 (a) C (b) B (c) A
2 B D E
3 (a) on Saturdays
(b) chatty
(c) homework
4 A C D
5 (a) A (b) B (c) A (d) C
6 (a) 60 (b) fish (c) 9.00 pm
7 (a) B (b) B (c) A
8 (a) by bus (b) loves (c) on foot (d) paper (e) nothing
9 B C D
10 (a) B (b) B (c) A (d) C
11 (a) i They are nice / kind ii (spent 3 hours on his) Maths homework
(b) Jade
dislikes: meals
likes: buildings
Pierre
likes: uniform
dislikes: start times / early start
12 1 Je **suis** assez **grand**.
2 J'ai **les** yeux **bruns**.
3 Mon **ami** est très **paresseux**.
4 Mon meilleur ami adore chanter.
5 Il est travailleur.
6 Demain, on va au parc ensemble.

122. Reading (Foundation)

1 (a) Clara (b) Enzo (c) Alex (d) Alex (e) Enzo (f) Clara
2 C D E
3 (a) i A ii C (b) B

4 (a) Emma
   Either lots of cars OR lots of noise
   Either streets aren't clean OR it's dangerous
   (b) Yanis
   recycle
   pollution
5 B C E
6 (a) students (b) won (c) next year
7 (a) i B ii B iii A iv A (b) C
8 (a) i by bus ii a book iii a dress (b) i C ii A
   (c) i give (her aunt) presents ii very happy
9 (a) travel, visit Africa (with friends)
   (b) get married, wants to have children / go to Canada on holiday, he likes snow
   (c) study languages / work in UK, good at English
10 (a) I like video games.
   (b) My brother uses social networks.
   (c) I hate watching films on TV.
   (d) Last Saturday I bought a new mobile.
   (e) If I have time I speak online.

127. Writing (Foundation)
1 Sample answers:
Il y a une famille.
On mange le déjeuner.
Je vois des fruits.
On boit.
2 Sample answer:
   (a) J'habite dans le nord de l'Angleterre dans une petite ville. J'aime ma ville car il y a beaucoup à faire. J'adore le cinéma et les magasins. Je vais aller en ville avec mes amis la semaine prochaine pour jouer au tennis.
   Sample answer:
   (b) J'ai un nouvel ordinateur portable Apple. Je l'adore parce qu'il est moderne et je l'utilise pour jouer à des jeux vidéo et envoyer des e-mails à mes amis. Le week-end prochain, je vais télécharger des chansons de mon chanteur préféré et je suis très content.
3 Sample answer:
   (a) Dans mon collège, les professeurs sont sympas et travailleurs. Je préfère mon professeur de maths car il m'aide beaucoup. J'aime mon école parce que les cours sont intéressants et on n'a pas trop de devoirs, mais je n'aime pas l'uniforme scolaire car ce n'est pas confortable. La semaine dernière, j'ai eu cours d'histoire, mais ce n'était pas bien car je ne m'entends pas bien avec mon professeur. J'ai aussi joué au foot dans un club. L'année prochaine, je vais aller au lycée étudier la science.
   Sample answer:
   (b) Dans ma famille, il y a quatre personnes: mon père, ma mère, mon frère qui s'appelle Louis, et moi. Ma mère travaille dans une banque et mon père est professeur. Je m'entends bien avec mon frère car il est très sympa, mais ma mère est trop stricte. La semaine dernière, je suis allé au bord de la mer avec ma famille. Nous avons joué au football sur la plage. Avant de rentrer, nous avons mangé un repas excellent dans un restaurant. Le week-end prochain, je vais faire du vélo avec mes amis.
4 (a) J'adore faire de l'exercice.
   (b) Mon sport préféré est le tennis.
   (c) J'aime aussi faire du vélo.
   (d) La semaine dernière, j'ai joué au basket dans le parc.
   (e) Je vais souvent à la piscine avec mon meilleur ami / ma meilleure amie.

129. Speaking (Higher)
1 Sample answers to follow-on questions:
   (a) J'aime jouer au foot avec ma famille.
   (b) J'aime le sport, surtout le tennis.

2 Sample answers:
   1 Bonjour. Qu'est-ce que vous voulez manger?
     Je voudrais des pâtes.
   2 D'accord. C'est tout?
     C'est combien, le poisson?
     Trois euros cinquante.
   3 Quel est votre boisson préférée?
     Je préfère l'eau.
   4 Vous avez des projets pour demain?
     Je vais visiter le musée demain.
   5 Vous avez une question?
     Le restaurant ouvre à quelle heure?
     A neuf heures et demie.

3 Sample answer:
Picture 1
Je vois quatre personnes à la campagne. Ils font du camping ensemble. Il y a le père qui a les cheveux noirs et il porte une chemise bleue. Il y a des arbres et le garçon à droite porte des baskets noires. On prépare un repas et on mange.
Picture 2
Il y a beaucoup de personnes dans un bus. Il y a deux personnes qui se parlent. Je crois qu'il fait froid car ils portent des vêtements chauds. La femme boit du café et elle a les cheveux longs et blonds. Le jeune homme a les cheveux noirs et il sourit.
Sample answers for follow-on questions:
Picture 1
(a) Je vais en France avec ma famille. C'est génial.
(b) J'ai visité un château et j'ai joué sur la plage.
Picture 2
(a) J'aime voyager en train car c'est rapide et pratique.
(b) Je suis allé en ville à pied. C'était excellent.

Travel and tourism
Est-ce que ta région est intéressante pour les touristes? Pourquoi ou Pourquoi pas?
Example of a grade 5–6 answer:
Ma région est intéressante pour les touristes car on peut y visiter le port historique et il y a un musée d'art moderne qui est vraiment intéressant pour tout le monde. Pour ceux qui aiment les magasins, on vient de construire un nouveau centre commercial où on peut acheter de tout.
Parle-moi d'une visite récente au parc / à la plage / à la campagne.
Example of a grade 7 answer: Récemment, je suis allé au bord de la mer où j'ai passé des heures sur la plage. Il a fait soleil, alors mon frère s'est reposé en lisant un livre pendant que ma sœur et moi avons passé des heures dans l'eau. C'était génial. Après ça, toute la famille est allée manger au restaurant et le repas était délicieux.
Comment est-ce que tu voudrais passer tes prochaines vacances?
Example of a grade 9 answer: Normalement, je passe mes vacances au bord de la mer dans le sud d'Angleterre avec mes parents et mon frère, mais l'année prochaine, nous allons visiter la France. Après avoir passé une nuit à Paris, nous avons l'intention de continuer notre voyage en voiture pour aller dans le sud du pays où nous allons passer deux semaines dans un hôtel que mon père a choisi. Avant de rentrer chez moi, j'essayerai les plats de la région et je parlerai aux gens en français. J'espère qu'on s'amusera bien ensemble!

131. Listening (Higher)
1 (a) B (b) B (c) A
2 (a) by bus (b) loves (c) on foot (d) paper (e) nothing
3 B C D
4 (a) B (b) B (c) A (d) C

5 (a) plastic bags (b) stop climate change
 (c) rubbish in streets / town
6 (a) fair (b) doesn't explain things (c) a different school
7 (a) Myriam: advantages: rest on beach; disadvantages: nothing to do in bad weather
 (b) Théo: advantages: less noise; disadvantages: poor transport
 (c) Chloé: advantages: taste a different culture; disadvantages: can't speak language / hard to speak to people
8 (a) i B ii C iii A
 (b) i B ii A iii B
9a B C E
9b i equality or liberty ii an organisation against racism and sexism iii changing the differences in men's and women's salaries for the same job iv a festival to celebrate French-speaking countries' cultures.
10 1 Dans ma **ville**, il y a une **mairie** et un **musée**.
 2 Les touristes **aiment nager** et se **détendre**.
 3 On peut aller au théâtre.
 4 Il fait souvent beau, surtout en été.
 5 Il faut goûter les **plats**.
 6 Je préfère vivre ici avec ma famille.

134. Reading (Higher)
1 (a) students (b) won (c) next year
2 (a) i B ii B iii A iv A (b) C
3 (a) i by bus ii a book iii a dress (b) i C ii A
 (c) i give (her aunt) presents ii very happy
4 (a) i perfect ii she has a ticket to see Michel
 (b) B
5 (a) B E F
 (b) i much too long / bad weather
  ii scared / frightened
  iii on the way to the hotel
  iv buy new clothes.
6 (a) A C
 (b) i lacked confidence
  ii 6 months
  iii proud
7 (a) i A ii B iii B
 (b) i The concerts are outside ii now
8 a watch what they eat and drink / do more physical exercise
 b he spent too much time in front of a screen
 c run
 d help others to follow a healthy diet / improve their families' fitness
 e explain the scientific link between unhealthy food and illness
9 I often help people in my neighbourhood. Later, I'd like to study law. My friends and I think that equality is important. I've already given money to poor people who live on my street. Next year I'll work for a charity which helps old people.

139. Writing (Higher)
1 Sample answer:
(a) Dans mon collège, les professeurs sont sympas et travailleurs. Je préfère mon professeur de maths car il m'aide beaucoup. J'aime mon école parce que les cours sont intéressants et on n'a pas trop de devoirs, mais je n'aime pas l'uniforme scolaire car ce n'est pas confortable. La semaine dernière, j'ai eu cours d'histoire, mais ce n'était pas bien car je ne m'entends pas bien avec mon professeur. J'ai aussi joué au foot dans un club. L'année prochaine, je vais aller au lycée pour étudier la science.
Sample answer:
(b) Dans ma famille, il y a quatre personnes: mon père, ma mère, mon frère qui s'appelle Louis, et moi. Ma mère travaille dans une banque et mon père est professeur. Je m'entends bien avec mon frère car il est très sympa, mais ma mère est trop stricte. La semaine dernière, je suis allé au bord de la mer avec ma famille. Nous avons joué au football sur la plage. Avant de rentrer, nous avons mangé un repas excellent dans un restaurant. Le week-end prochain, je vais faire du vélo avec mes amis.
2 Sample answer:
(a) Selon moi, les vacances sont importantes car il faut essayer d'oublier ses soucis de tous les jours. Alors, on passe de bonnes vacances quand on peut se reposer et qu'on ne doit pas travailler. À mon avis, aller à l'étranger est un moyen excellent de découvrir un autre pays et une autre culture car c'est vraiment intéressant, mais, par contre, parfois, il est difficile de s'exprimer quand on ne parle pas la langue du pays.
L'année dernière, je suis allé en vacances dans le sud de la France et c'était génial. Ma sœur et moi avons fait de la natation dans la mer chaude et on s'est bien amusés. Mes parents ont décidé de passer des heures dans un château, ce qui était intéressant pour eux. Ils ont aussi visité un musée d'art, mais ils ont dit que c'était nul. L'année prochaine, j'irai au Canada visiter ma tante qui y habite, et j'espère que ce sera amusant.
(b) Je crois que les réseaux sociaux sont intéressants car on peut lire les avis des autres et on peut aussi s'informer. Avant, je pensais qu'il n'y avait que des avantages à la technologie car j'adore parler et jouer avec mes copains en ligne, mais maintenant, je sais qu'il y a des inconvénients comme le harcèlement et la cybercriminalité. La semaine dernière, j'ai téléchargé de la musique, ce qui était excellent, car j'ai pu trouver des chansons que j'aime beaucoup. J'ai aussi envoyé des e-mails à une copine qui habite en Afrique et j'ai passé des heures sur mon réseau social préféré qui s'appelle Instagram. La semaine prochaine, je vais faire des recherches en ligne pour mes devoirs, j'achèterai des vêtements sur Internet et je chercherai un cadeau pour l'anniversaire de mon frère qui aura bientôt quinze ans.
3 J'aime faire les magasins en ville. Ma sœur vient souvent avec moi. Je voyage toujours en bus ou en train. Le mois dernier, j'ai acheté une jupe et des baskets en ligne. Mes amis / copains vont aller à un nouveau centre commercial le week-end prochain parce qu'ils veulent trouver un cadeau pour mon anniversaire.